The Dr. Now

1200-Calorie Diet Plan

for Beginners

Delicious, Easy, and Nutrient-Packed Low-Carb Recipes for Calorie Control and Better Health | Perfect for Novice Seeking Simple, Flavorful Meals

Jessica Macdonald

Contents

Introduction

The Dr. Now 1200-Calorie Diet is a scientifically designed, calorie-controlled eating plan aimed at promoting sustainable weight loss and improved metabolic health. Created by renowned bariatric surgeon Dr. Nowzaradan, this diet emphasizes portion control, nutrient-dense foods, and balanced macronutrients to help individuals achieve their health goals without feeling deprived.

The Dr. Now 1200-Calorie Diet Plan for Beginners is your comprehensive guide to adopting a low-calorie, high-nutrient diet designed for sustainable weight loss and overall health improvement. Inspired by Dr. Nowzaradan's medical weight loss program, this cookbook provides you with everything you need to start your weight loss journey, including simple, flavorful, and balanced meals that are perfect for maintaining a 1200-calorie daily intake. Whether you're looking to shed pounds, improve your eating habits, or maintain long-term health, this plan is designed to guide you through the process.

Inside this cookbook, you will find 1200-calorie meal options ranging from tasty breakfasts to hearty lunches and satisfying dinners, all made with easy-to-find ingredients. The diet emphasizes healthy, whole foods such as lean proteins, vegetables, and healthy fats while limiting processed foods and excess sugars. The goal is to reduce body fat, increase energy, and improve overall well-being.

With clear instructions and step-by-step recipes, this book empowers you to take control of your health and achieve your weight loss goals. Whether you're new to dieting or looking for a structured plan, the Dr. Now 1200-Calorie Diet Plan for Beginners offers a practical approach to eating better and feeling great every day. Start your journey today, and unlock the potential of healthy eating for lasting results.

The Dr. Now 1200-Calorie Diet is built on three core principles:

1. Calorie Control: Limiting daily intake to 1200 calories creates a calorie deficit, essential for weight loss.

2. Nutrient Density: Focus on whole, unprocessed foods like lean proteins, vegetables, and healthy fats to meet nutritional needs.

3. Sustainability: Simple, satisfying meals prevent burnout and make long-term adherence achievable.

This diet is not just about cutting calories—it's about making every calorie count. By prioritizing high-quality ingredients and balanced meals, it ensures you stay energized and nourished while shedding pounds.

What Is Dr. Now 1200-Calorie Diet Plan?

The Dr. Now 1200-Calorie Diet is a structured eating plan designed to help individuals lose weight safely and effectively. Rooted in medical science, it was developed by Dr. Nowzaradan, a leading expert in weight management and bariatric surgery. The diet restricts daily calorie intake to 1200 calories, a level proven to promote weight loss while minimizing muscle loss and metabolic slowdown.

Unlike fad diets, this plan emphasizes balanced nutrition, incorporating lean proteins, complex carbs, and healthy fats to keep you full and energized. It also encourages mindful eating habits, such as portion control and regular meal timing, to foster a healthier relationship with food. Perfect for beginners, the diet is flexible and adaptable, offering options for various dietary preferences, including vegetarian and low-carb variations. With its focus on simplicity and sustainability, the Dr. Now 1200-Calorie Diet is more than a diet—it's a lifestyle change that empowers you to take control of your health.

The Science Behind the 1200-Calorie Diet

The Dr. Now 1200-Calorie Diet is rooted in the science of calorie deficit and metabolic health. By limiting daily intake to 1200 calories, the diet creates a sustainable energy deficit, encouraging the body to burn stored fat for fuel. This approach is particularly effective for individuals with sedentary lifestyles or those needing significant weight loss, as it balances calorie restriction with essential nutrient intake to prevent metabolic slowdown.

Why 1200 Calories? Metabolic Basics for Safe Weight Loss

A 1200-calorie daily intake is carefully chosen to promote weight loss without pushing the body into "starvation mode." For most adults, this level creates a deficit of 500-1000 calories per day, leading to a safe and steady weight loss of 1-2 pounds per week. This gradual approach helps preserve muscle mass, maintain energy levels, and reduce the risk of nutrient deficiencies. Additionally, 1200 calories is low enough to trigger fat burning but high enough to provide the energy needed for daily activities.

How Dr. Now's Plan Balances Macronutrients (Carbs/Protein/Fat)

The diet emphasizes a balanced macronutrient ratio to optimize satiety, energy, and overall health:

- **Protein:** High-protein foods like lean meats, eggs, and legumes are prioritized to support muscle repair, boost metabolism, and keep you feeling full longer.
- **Carbohydrates:** Complex carbs from vegetables, whole grains, and fruits provide steady energy and fiber, aiding digestion and preventing blood sugar spikes.
- **Fats:** Healthy fats from sources like avocado, nuts, and olive oil are included in moderation to support hormone production and nutrient absorption.

This balance ensures that even at a lower calorie intake, your body receives the fuel it needs to function optimally.

Avoiding Nutrient Deficiencies: Key Vitamins & Minerals to Prioritize

A 1200-calorie diet requires careful planning to avoid deficiencies. Dr. Now's plan focuses on nutrient-dense foods to meet daily requirements:

- **Vitamins:** Leafy greens, citrus fruits, and fortified foods provide essential vitamins like A, C, and D.
- **Minerals:** Lean meats, dairy, and legumes supply iron, calcium, and magnesium, while nuts and seeds offer zinc and selenium.
- **Fiber:** Whole grains, vegetables, and fruits ensure adequate fiber intake for digestive health.

By prioritizing these nutrients, the diet supports overall well-being while promoting weight loss, making it a safe and effective choice for beginners.

Benefits of the Dr. Now 1200-Calorie Diet Plan

The Dr. Now 1200-Calorie Diet Plan offers numerous benefits for individuals looking to lose weight, improve their eating habits, and boost their overall health. Designed with the goal of sustainable, long-term weight loss, this diet plan provides a structured, calorie-restricted approach that is easy to follow. Here are some of the key benefits:

1. **Effective Weight Loss:** By reducing daily calorie intake to 1200 calories, the Dr. Now 1200-Calorie Diet encourages the body to burn stored fat for energy, leading to consistent and sustainable weight loss. It helps individuals achieve their weight loss goals by creating a calorie deficit without feeling deprived.
2. **Balanced Nutrition:** Despite its calorie restrictions, this diet emphasizes nutrient-dense foods, ensuring that you receive adequate vitamins, minerals, and fiber. Lean proteins, vegetables, and healthy fats are incorporated into meals to provide balanced nutrition that supports metabolism and overall health.
3. **Improved Metabolism:** By focusing on protein-rich foods, the Dr. Now diet helps maintain lean muscle mass while promoting fat loss. It increases metabolic rate, making it easier to burn calories even at rest.
4. **Reduced Hunger and Cravings:** The inclusion of fiber and protein in the diet helps control appetite, keeping you fuller for longer. This leads to fewer cravings and reduced overeating, which is a major obstacle in many weight-loss programs.
5. **Blood Sugar Regulation:** The Dr. Now diet limits sugar and refined carbohydrates, which helps stabilize blood sugar levels. This is particularly beneficial for individuals with type 2 diabetes or those at risk of developing it.
6. **Long-Term Health Benefits:** By focusing on whole foods and limiting processed, high-calorie items, the Dr. Now 1200-Calorie Diet can improve heart health, reduce cholesterol levels, and support overall well-being. It encourages a healthy relationship with food and promotes a sustainable, healthy lifestyle.

In summary, the Dr. Now 1200-Calorie Diet is a structured, balanced approach to weight loss that not only helps shed pounds but also improves overall health, boosts metabolism, and encourages long-term dietary changes. It's ideal for anyone looking for a safe and effective way to manage their weight and improve their health.

What Food to Eat

The Dr. Now 1200-Calorie Diet Plan emphasizes healthy, nutrient-dense foods to help you stay full, energized, and satisfied while losing weight. Here's what to eat on the plan:

1. **Lean Proteins:** Chicken breast, turkey, fish (salmon, tuna, etc.), and lean cuts of beef provide essential protein for muscle maintenance and satiety.
2. **Non-Starchy Vegetables:** Fill your plate with vegetables like spinach, broccoli, kale, cauliflower, and zucchini. These are low in calories but high in vitamins, minerals, and fiber.
3. **Healthy Fats:** Include moderate amounts of healthy fats such as avocado, olive oil, and nuts. These fats support overall health and help with fullness.
4. **Fruits:** Fresh fruits like berries, apples, and pears are nutrient-packed and satisfy your sweet cravings with natural sugars.
5. **Whole Grains:** Choose small portions of whole grains like quinoa, brown rice, and oatmeal for energy and fiber.

These foods provide the necessary nutrition while maintaining a calorie deficit for weight loss.

What Food to Avoid

To maximize the effectiveness of the Dr. Now 1200-Calorie Diet, it's essential to avoid foods that are high in empty calories, added sugars, and unhealthy fats. Here's a quick guide:

1. **Sugary Foods:** Avoid candies, sodas, pastries, and sugary cereals. These spike blood sugar levels and provide little nutritional value.
2. **Processed Snacks:** Chips, crackers, and packaged baked goods are often high in calories, sodium, and unhealthy fats.

3. **Fried Foods:** French fries, fried chicken, and other deep-fried items are calorie-dense and can derail your progress.
4. **High-Calorie Beverages:** Skip sugary coffee drinks, energy drinks, and alcohol, as they add unnecessary calories without filling you up.
5. **Refined Carbs:** White bread, white rice, and pasta lack fiber and can cause energy crashes. Opt for whole-grain alternatives instead.
6. **High-Fat Dairy:** Limit full-fat cheese, cream, and butter, as they are calorie-heavy. Choose low-fat or non-dairy options.

By avoiding these foods, you'll stay within your calorie limit while focusing on nutrient-dense, satisfying options that support your weight loss goals.

Getting Started: Your First 7 Days

Embarking on the Dr. Now 1200-Calorie Diet can feel overwhelming, but with a clear plan, your first week can set the tone for long-term success. Here's a step-by-step guide to help you navigate the initial phase with confidence.

Step-by-Step Meal Prep Guide for Beginners

1. Day 1-2: Plan Your Meals
Use the cookbook's 7-day meal plan or create your own using the provided recipes.
Focus on simple, repeatable meals to minimize stress. For example, oatmeal for breakfast, grilled chicken salad for lunch, and roasted veggies with quinoa for dinner.

2. Day 3: Grocery Shopping
Stick to your list to avoid impulse buys. Prioritize fresh produce, lean proteins, and whole grains.

3. Day 4: Batch Cooking
Prepare staples like grilled chicken, hard-boiled eggs, and roasted vegetables in bulk. Store them in portioned containers for easy access.

4. Day 5-7: Daily Assembly
Combine prepped ingredients into meals. For example, toss pre-cooked chicken with greens and a light dressing for a quick salad.

By breaking down the process, meal prep becomes manageable and less intimidating.

Sample Grocery List: Budget-Friendly Staples

Here's a starter list to stock your kitchen without breaking the bank:
- **Proteins:** Eggs, chicken breast, canned tuna, tofu, Greek yogurt.
- **Vegetables:** Spinach, broccoli, carrots, zucchini, frozen mixed veggies.
- **Fruits:** Apples, bananas, berries, oranges.
- **Grains:** Brown rice, quinoa, whole-grain bread, oats.
- **Pantry Staples:** Olive oil, canned beans, spices, low-sodium broth.

These items are versatile, affordable, and form the foundation of countless 1200-calorie meals.

Kitchen Tools You'll Need (No Fancy Gadgets Required)

You don't need a fully stocked kitchen to succeed. Here are the essentials:
1. **Chef's Knife and Cutting Board:** For chopping veggies and proteins.
2. **Non-Stick Skillet:** Perfect for cooking eggs, sautéing vegetables, or searing chicken.
3. **Baking Sheet:** Great for roasting veggies or baking fish.
4. **Measuring Cups and Spoons:** Ensure accurate portion control.
5. **Food Storage Containers:** Keep prepped ingredients fresh and organized.

With these tools, you can whip up delicious, calorie-controlled meals without investing in expensive equipment.

Meal Timing and Portion Control

Mastering meal timing and portion control is key to success on the Dr. Now 1200-Calorie Diet. These strategies help manage hunger, maintain energy levels, and ensure you stay within your daily calorie limit. Here's how to make them work for you:

Intermittent Fasting vs. Small Frequent Meals: What Works Best?

- **Intermittent Fasting (IF):** This approach involves eating within a specific time window (e.g., 8 hours) and fasting for the remaining 16 hours. It can simplify calorie control by reducing the number of meals you plan and eat. However, it may not suit everyone, especially those who feel fatigued or irritable without regular meals.
- **Small Frequent Meals:** Eating 4-6 smaller meals throughout the day can help stabilize blood sugar levels and curb cravings. This approach is ideal for individuals who prefer consistent energy and enjoy variety in their meals.

The best choice depends on your lifestyle and preferences. Experiment with both

to see what keeps you satisfied and energized.

Visual Portion Guides (e.g., "Your Protein Should Fit Your Palm")

Portion control doesn't require a food scale—use these simple visual cues:

- **Protein:** A serving of meat, fish, or tofu should be about the size of your palm (3-4 ounces).
- **Carbs:** A portion of rice, pasta, or potatoes should fit in your cupped hand (about ½ cup cooked).
- **Fats:** A serving of nuts or cheese should be roughly the size of your thumb (1 tablespoon or 1 ounce).
- **Vegetables:** Fill half your plate with non-starchy veggies like spinach, broccoli, or zucchini.

These guidelines make it easy to estimate portions without counting every calorie.

Hydration Tips: How Water Supports Calorie Control

Staying hydrated is crucial for weight loss and overall health. Here's why:

- **Curbs Hunger:** Thirst is often mistaken for hunger. Drinking a glass of water before meals can help you eat less.
- **Boosts Metabolism:** Proper hydration supports your body's ability to burn calories efficiently.
- **Reduces Bloating:** Water helps flush out excess sodium, reducing water retention and bloating.

Aim for at least 8 cups (64 ounces) of water daily. Add flavor with lemon slices, cucumber, or mint to make hydration more enjoyable.

By combining smart meal timing, portion control, and hydration, you'll maximize the effectiveness of the Dr. Now 1200-Calorie Diet while feeling satisfied and energized throughout the day.

Overcoming Common Challenges

The Dr. Now 1200-Calorie Diet is designed to be sustainable, but like any diet, it comes with challenges. Here's how to tackle the most common hurdles and stay on track:

Battling Hunger: High-Fiber & High-Protein Hacks

Hunger is a natural response to calorie restriction, but you can manage it effectively:

- **High-Fiber Foods:** Incorporate fiber-rich options like vegetables, fruits, and whole grains. Fiber slows digestion, keeping you fuller longer. For example, add spinach to your omelet or snack on an apple with almond butter.
- **High-Protein Meals:** Protein is highly satiating and helps preserve muscle mass. Include lean proteins like chicken, fish, eggs, or tofu in every meal. A protein-packed breakfast, such as Greek yogurt with berries, can curb mid-morning cravings.
- **Hydration:** Sometimes thirst mimics hunger. Drink a glass of water before reaching for a snack.

These strategies help you feel satisfied while staying within your calorie limit.

Social Situations: Dining Out and Family Gatherings

Navigating social events can be tricky, but with a little planning, you can stay on track:

- **Dining Out:** Check the menu online beforehand and choose grilled, baked, or steamed options. Ask for dressings and sauces on the side, and avoid fried or creamy dishes.
- **Family Gatherings:** Offer to bring a healthy dish, like a vegetable platter or a light salad, to ensure there's something you can enjoy. Focus on portion control and savor each bite.
- **Mindful Eating:** Eat slowly and enjoy the conversation. This helps you recognize when you're full and avoid overeating.

By planning ahead and making mindful choices, you can enjoy social events without derailing your progress.

Managing Energy Slumps: Smart Snack Swaps

Low energy is a common complaint on calorie-restricted diets, but the right snacks can help:

- **Healthy Carbs:** Pair complex carbs with protein for sustained energy. Try hummus with carrot sticks or a small handful of nuts with a piece of fruit.
- **Low-Calorie Boosters:** Snack on air-popped popcorn, rice cakes, or a hard-boiled egg for a quick pick-me-up.
- **Timing Matters:** Eat a small snack before your energy typically dips, like mid-morning or mid-afternoon.

These swaps keep your energy stable without exceeding your calorie limit.

By addressing hunger, social pressures, and energy slumps with practical solutions, you'll find it easier to stick to the Dr. Now 1200-Calorie Diet and achieve your weight loss goals.

Exercise Synergy: Moving Without Overeating

When following a 1200-calorie diet, exercise can be a powerful tool for maintaining energy levels and supporting weight loss. However, it's crucial to strike a balance between moving enough to stay active and avoiding the temptation to overeat as a reward for working out. Low-intensity workouts, such as walking, yoga, or light cycling, are excellent options for 1200-calorie dieters because they burn calories without significantly increasing hunger. On the other hand, High-Intensity Interval Training (HIIT) can be effective for maximizing calorie burn in a short time, but it may also spike appetite, making it harder to stick to a low-calorie plan. The key is to listen to your body and choose workouts that align with your energy levels and hunger cues.

After exercising, refueling with a 100-calorie snack can help replenish energy without derailing your diet. Opt for nutrient-dense options like a small apple with a teaspoon of peanut butter, a hard-boiled egg, or a handful of almonds. These choices provide protein, healthy fats, and fiber to keep you satisfied.

One common pitfall is falling into the "I exercised, so I can eat more" mindset. To avoid this, remind yourself that exercise is a complement to your diet, not a license to overindulge. Track your calories diligently and focus on nourishing your body with wholesome foods rather than using workouts as an excuse to consume extra calories.

Transitioning to Maintenance: Life After 1200 Calories

After successfully losing weight on a 1200-calorie diet, transitioning to maintenance can feel daunting. The key is to avoid sudden jumps in calorie intake, which can lead to rebound weight gain. Reverse dieting—a gradual increase in calories—can help your metabolism adjust without causing rapid weight regain. Start by adding 100-200 calories per week, focusing on whole foods like lean proteins, whole grains, and healthy fats.

Mindful eating habits are essential for long-term success. Practice eating slowly, savoring each bite, and paying attention to hunger and fullness cues. These habits can help you maintain your weight without feeling deprived.

It's also important to recognize when to adjust your calorie intake. If you're feeling fatigued, experiencing frequent hunger, or hitting a plateau in your fitness goals, it may be time to reassess your caloric needs. Consulting a nutritionist can provide personalized guidance to ensure you're fueling your body appropriately while maintaining your hard-earned progress.

Useful Tips of the Dr. Now 1200-Calorie Diet Plan

The Dr. Now 1200-Calorie Diet Plan offers a structured approach to weight loss, and to make the most out of it, here are some helpful tips:

1. **Meal Prep for Success:** Plan and prepare your meals in advance. By spending time on weekends or during your free time prepping meals, you can avoid the temptation of unhealthy food choices during the week. Pre-portioning meals into containers also helps manage calorie intake more effectively.

2. **Focus on Lean Proteins:** Incorporating lean protein sources like chicken, turkey, and fish into your meals is key. Protein helps keep you full and satisfied, preventing overeating. It also supports muscle maintenance while you're losing weight.

3. **Increase Vegetable Intake:** Non-starchy vegetables like leafy greens, bell peppers, and zucchini should make up a significant portion of your meals. They're low in calories but high in nutrients, ensuring that you're getting vitamins and fiber while staying full.

4. **Stay Hydrated:** Drinking enough water is vital. Water not only helps with digestion but can also curb hunger and keep you feeling full. Aim for at least 8 glasses of water a day, and consider incorporating herbal teas for variety.

5. **Track Your Calories:** While the plan focuses on a 1200-calorie daily intake, it's important to track your calories accurately. Use a food journal or an app to monitor your intake to ensure you're sticking to your calorie goals.

6. **Listen to Your Body:** Pay attention to how your body responds to the diet. If you feel overly hungry, tired, or weak, consider adjusting portion sizes or consulting a professional to ensure you're meeting all your nutritional needs.

7. **Exercise Regularly:** While the Dr. Now diet plan focuses on food, regular exercise will amplify results. Aim for a mix of cardio and strength training to support fat loss and overall health.

By following these tips, you can stay on track, avoid common pitfalls, and see the best results with the Dr. Now 1200-Calorie Diet Plan.

To make The Dr. Now 1200-Calorie Diet Plan for Beginners the ultimate resource for weight loss success, we've included 5 exclusive bonuses that provide additional tools, strategies, and support. These bonuses are designed to enhance the core content of the book, making it easier for you to stay on track, build healthy habits, and achieve your goals. Here's a detailed look at what each bonus includes:

Bonus 1: 7-Day Meal Prep Guide with Shopping Lists

Meal prepping is one of the most effective ways to stick to a 1200-calorie diet, and this bonus takes the stress out of planning and preparation. The 7-Day Meal Prep Guide includes:
Daily meal plans: Breakfast, lunch, dinner, and snacks that are perfectly portioned and calorie-controlled.
This 7-Day Meal Prep Guide is designed to help you stay on track with the Dr. Now 1200-Calorie Diet Plan by providing balanced, calorie-controlled meals that are easy to prepare and delicious to eat. Each day includes breakfast, lunch, dinner, and two snacks, along with a detailed shopping list to make grocery shopping a breeze. Let's dive in!

Day 1: Monday
Breakfast: Spinach and Mushroom Omelet
2 eggs, 1 cup spinach, ½ cup mushrooms, 1 tsp olive oil (250 calories).
Snack: Apple with Peanut Butter
1 small apple, 1 tbsp peanut butter (100 calories).
Lunch: Grilled Chicken Salad
3 oz grilled chicken, 2 cups mixed greens, ½ cup cherry tomatoes, 1 tbsp light vinaigrette (300 calories).
Snack: Carrot Sticks with Hummus
1 cup carrot sticks, 2 tbsp hummus (80 calories).
Dinner: Baked Cod with Roasted Vegetables
4 oz cod, 1 cup roasted zucchini and bell peppers, ½ cup quinoa (350 calories).
Shopping List for Day 1
Produce: Spinach, mushrooms, apple, mixed greens, cherry tomatoes, carrots, zucchini, bell peppers.
Proteins: Eggs, chicken breast, cod.
Pantry: Olive oil, peanut butter, light vinaigrette, hummus, quinoa.

Day 2: Tuesday
Breakfast: Greek Yogurt Parfait
½ cup non-fat Greek yogurt, ½ cup berries, 1 tbsp granola (200 calories).
Snack: Hard-Boiled Egg
1 hard-boiled egg (70 calories).
Lunch: Turkey Wrap
3 oz turkey breast, 1 whole-grain tortilla, 1 cup lettuce, ½ cup cucumber slices, 1 tsp mustard (300 calories).
Snack: Mixed Nuts
1 oz mixed nuts (160 calories).
Dinner: Grilled Shrimp with Cauliflower Rice
4 oz shrimp, 1 cup cauliflower rice, ½ cup steamed broccoli (350 calories).
Shopping List for Day 2
Produce: Berries, lettuce, cucumber, broccoli.
Proteins: Greek yogurt, turkey breast, shrimp.
Pantry: Granola, whole-grain tortilla, mustard, mixed nuts, cauliflower rice.

Day 3: Wednesday
Breakfast: Overnight Oats
½ cup rolled oats, ½ cup almond milk, 1 tbsp chia seeds, ½ cup blueberries (250 calories).
Snack: Celery with Almond Butter
1 cup celery sticks, 1 tbsp almond butter (100 calories).
Lunch: Tuna Salad
3 oz canned tuna (in water), 1 cup mixed greens, ½ cup cucumber, 1 tbsp light mayo (300 calories).
Snack: Cottage Cheese with Pineapple
½ cup low-fat cottage cheese, ½ cup pineapple chunks (120 calories).
Dinner: Grilled Chicken with Sweet Potato
4 oz grilled chicken, ½ medium sweet potato, 1 cup steamed green beans (350 calories).
Shopping List for Day 3
Produce: Blueberries, celery, mixed greens, cucumber, pineapple, green beans, sweet potato.
Proteins: Rolled oats, almond milk, tuna, chicken breast, cottage cheese.
Pantry: Chia seeds, almond butter, light mayo.

Day 4: Thursday
Breakfast: Avocado Toast
1 slice whole-grain bread, ¼ avocado, 1 poached egg (250 calories).
Snack: Greek Yogurt with Honey
½ cup non-fat Greek yogurt, 1 tsp honey (100 calories).
Lunch: Quinoa Salad
½ cup quinoa, ½ cup chickpeas, 1 cup mixed veggies (cucumber, tomato, bell pepper), 1 tbsp lemon dressing (300 calories).
Snack: Edamame
½ cup steamed edamame (120 calories).
Dinner: Baked Salmon with Asparagus
4 oz salmon, 1 cup roasted asparagus, ½ cup brown rice (350 calories).
Shopping List for Day 4
Produce: Avocado, mixed veggies (cucumber, tomato, bell pepper), asparagus.
Proteins: Whole-grain bread, eggs, Greek yogurt, chickpeas, salmon.
Pantry: Quinoa, honey, lemon dressing, edamame, brown rice.

Day 5: Friday
Breakfast: Smoothie Bowl
½ banana, ½ cup spinach, ½ cup almond milk, 1 tbsp protein powder, 1 tbsp granola (250 calories).
Snack: Rice Cake with Almond Butter
1 rice cake, 1 tbsp almond butter (100 calories).
Lunch: Grilled Chicken Wrap
3 oz grilled chicken, 1 whole-grain tortilla, 1 cup lettuce, ½ cup salsa (300 calories).
Snack: Baby Carrots with Guacamole
1 cup baby carrots, 2 tbsp guacamole (80 calories).
Dinner: Turkey Meatballs with Zoodles
4 oz turkey meatballs, 1 cup zucchini noodles, ½ cup marinara sauce (350 calories).
Shopping List for Day 5
Produce: Banana, spinach, lettuce, baby carrots, zucchini.
Proteins: Almond milk, protein powder, chicken breast, turkey meatballs.
Pantry: Granola, rice cake, almond butter, salsa, guacamole, marinara sauce.

Day 6: Saturday
Breakfast: Veggie Scramble
2 eggs, ½ cup bell peppers, ½ cup onions, 1 tsp olive oil (250 calories).
Snack: Cottage Cheese with Berries
½ cup low-fat cottage cheese, ½ cup strawberries (100 calories).
Lunch: Grilled Shrimp Salad
4 oz shrimp, 2 cups mixed greens, ½ cup cherry tomatoes, 1 tbsp light dressing (300 calories).
Snack: Dark Chocolate
1 square dark chocolate (70 calories).
Dinner: Grilled Chicken with Mashed Cauliflower
4 oz grilled chicken, 1 cup mashed cauliflower, ½ cup steamed carrots (350 calories).
Shopping List for Day 6
Produce: Bell peppers, onions, mixed greens, cherry tomatoes, strawberries, carrots.
Proteins: Eggs, shrimp, chicken breast, cottage cheese.
Pantry: Olive oil, light dressing, dark chocolate, cauliflower.

Day 7: Sunday
Breakfast: Protein Pancakes
2 small protein pancakes, 1 tbsp sugar-free syrup, ½ cup berries (250 calories).
Snack: Hard-Boiled Egg
1 hard-boiled egg (70 calories).
Lunch: Grilled Turkey Burger
3 oz turkey patty, 1 whole-grain bun, 1 cup lettuce, ½ cup cucumber slices (300 calories).
Snack: Mixed Nuts
1 oz mixed nuts (160 calories).
Dinner: Baked Cod with Roasted Veggies
4 oz cod, 1 cup roasted Brussels sprouts, ½ cup quinoa (350 calories).
Shopping List for Day 7
Produce: Berries, lettuce, cucumber, Brussels sprouts.
Proteins: Protein pancake mix, turkey patty, cod.
Pantry: Sugar-free syrup, whole-grain bun, mixed nuts, quinoa.
This guide ensures you have delicious, nutrient-dense meals ready to go, even on your busiest days. It's the perfect tool to help you stay consistent and avoid the temptation of unhealthy convenience foods.

Bonus 2: Exercise Synergy: Low-Impact Workouts for Beginners

If you're following a low-calorie diet like the Dr. Now 1200-Calorie Plan, low-impact exercises are a great way to stay active without overexerting yourself. These workouts are gentle on your joints, help burn calories, and improve overall fitness. Here's a simple, beginner-friendly routine you can do at home or outdoors:
1. Walking (30 Minutes)
How to do it: Start with a brisk walk at a pace that feels comfortable but slightly challenging.
Tips: Use proper walking shoes, maintain good posture, and swing your arms naturally.
Calories burned: ~150-200 calories.
2. Bodyweight Squats (2 Sets of 10-12 Reps)
How to do it: Stand with feet shoulder-width apart. Lower your body as if sitting in a chair, keeping your knees behind your toes. Return to standing.
Tips: Keep your chest up and engage your core.
Calories burned: ~50-70 calories.
3. Wall Push-Ups (2 Sets of 10-12 Reps)
How to do it: Stand facing a wall, place your hands on it at shoulder height, and perform push-ups by bending your elbows.
Tips: Keep your body straight and move slowly.
Calories burned: ~30-50 calories.
4. Seated Leg Lifts (2 Sets of 10-12 Reps per Leg)
How to do it: Sit on a chair with your back straight. Lift one leg at a time, hold for 2 seconds, and lower it.
Tips: Engage your core and avoid swinging your legs.
Calories burned: ~30-50 calories.
5. Stretching (5-10 Minutes)
How to do it: Stretch your hamstrings, quads, shoulders, and back. Hold each stretch for 20-30 seconds.
Tips: Breathe deeply and avoid bouncing.
Calories burned: ~20-30 calories.
Total Calories burned: ~280-400 calories.
This low-impact routine is perfect for beginners and complements a low-calorie diet by boosting energy and supporting weight loss without overexertion. Start with 3-4 days a week and gradually increase as you build strength and endurance!

Whether you're new to exercise or returning after a break, this bonus provides the tools to create a sustainable fitness habit that supports your weight loss goals.

Bonus 3: Mindful Eating Mastery: A 21-Day Challenge

This challenge will help you build a healthier relationship with food, stay within your calorie limit, and enjoy every bite. Follow these daily steps:

Week 1: Foundation
Day 1-3: Eat without distractions (no TV or phones).
Day 4-7: Chew each bite 15-20 times and savor the flavors.

Week 2: Awareness
Day 8-10: Pause halfway through meals to check hunger levels.
Day 11-14: Use a smaller plate and portion meals mindfully.

Week 3: Habits
Day 15-17: Eat slowly, taking at least 20 minutes per meal.
Day 18-21: Practice gratitude before eating—reflect on where your food came from.

Daily Tips:
1. Drink water before meals to avoid mistaking thirst for hunger.
2. Stop eating when you're 80% full.
3. Journal about your hunger cues and emotions after meals.
This challenge will help you stay on track with your 1200-calorie diet while fostering mindful, intentional eating habits!

Bonus 4: Post-Workout Recovery: 100-Calorie Snack Recipes

Refueling after exercise is essential, but it's easy to overdo it on calories. This bonus provides 10 quick and easy 100-calorie snack recipes that are perfect for post-workout recovery, including:
Here are 10 delicious, easy-to-make snacks that are perfect for post-workout recovery and fit seamlessly into a 1200-calorie diet. Each recipe is around 100 calories and packed with nutrients to refuel your body.

Greek Yogurt with Berries
Prep Time: 2 minutes | Cook Time: 0 minutes | Serves: 1
½ cup non-fat Greek yogurt
¼ cup fresh berries (e.g., blueberries or strawberries)
1. Combine the Greek yogurt and berries in a small bowl.
2. Enjoy immediately for a refreshing, protein-packed snack.
Per Serving: Calories 100; Fat 0.2g; Sodium 50mg; Carbs 12g; Fiber 1.5g; Sugar 8g; Protein 12g

Hard-Boiled Egg with Cucumber Slices
Prep Time: 5 minutes | Cook Time: 10 minutes | Serves: 1
1 hard-boiled egg
½ cup cucumber slices
1. Slice the hard-boiled egg and cucumber.
2. Arrange on a plate and enjoy as a light, protein-rich snack.
Per Serving: Calories 100; Fat 5g; Sodium 70mg; Carbs 2g; Fiber 0.5g; Sugar 1g; Protein 8g

Apple Slices with Almond Butter
Prep Time: 5 minutes | Cook Time: 0 minutes | Serves: 1
½ small apple, sliced
1 tsp almond butter
1. Spread almond butter on apple slices.
2. Enjoy the perfect balance of sweet and savory.
Per Serving: Calories 100; Fat 4g; Sodium 0mg; Carbs 15g; Fiber 2g; Sugar 10g; Protein 1g

Cottage Cheese with Pineapple
Prep Time: 2 minutes | Cook Time: 0 minutes | Serves: 1
¼ cup low-fat cottage cheese
¼ cup pineapple chunks
1. Combine cottage cheese and pineapple in a bowl.
2. Enjoy a creamy, tropical snack.
Per Serving: Calories 100; Fat 1g; Sodium 200mg; Carbs 12g; Fiber 1g; Sugar 9g; Protein 8g

Rice Cake with Hummus
Prep Time: 2 minutes | Cook Time: 0 minutes | Serves: 1
1 plain rice cake
1 tbsp hummus
1. Spread hummus on the rice cake.
2. Enjoy a crunchy, satisfying snack.
Per Serving: Calories 100; Fat 3g; Sodium 100mg; Carbs 15g; Fiber 1g; Sugar 1g; Protein 2g

Turkey Roll-Ups
Prep Time: 5 minutes | Cook Time: 0 minutes | Serves: 1
2 slices turkey breast
1 lettuce leaf
1. Wrap the turkey slices around the lettuce leaf.
2. Roll up and enjoy a protein-packed snack.
Per Serving: Calories 100; Fat 1g; Sodium 300mg; Carbs 1g; Fiber 0g; Sugar 0g; Protein 18g

Edamame
Prep Time: 2 minutes | Cook Time: 5 minutes | Serves: 1
½ cup steamed edamame (in pods)
1. Steam edamame until tender.
2. Sprinkle with a pinch of salt and enjoy.
Per Serving: Calories 100; Fat 3g; Sodium 5mg; Carbs 8g; Fiber 4g; Sugar 2g; Protein 9g

Dark Chocolate and Almonds
Prep Time: 2 minutes | Cook Time: 0 minutes | Serves: 1
1 square dark chocolate (70%+)
3 almonds
1. Pair the dark chocolate with almonds.
2. Enjoy a sweet and satisfying treat.
Per Serving: Calories 100; Fat 7g; Sodium 0mg; Carbs 6g; Fiber 1g; Sugar 4g; Protein 2g

Carrot Sticks with Guacamole
Prep Time: 5 minutes | Cook Time: 0 minutes | Serves: 1
1 cup carrot sticks
1 tbsp guacamole
1. Dip carrot sticks into guacamole.
2. Enjoy a crunchy, nutrient-rich snack.
Per Serving: Calories 100; Fat 5g; Sodium 50mg; Carbs 12g; Fiber 4g; Sugar 6g; Protein 1g

Protein Bites
Prep Time: 10 minutes | Cook Time: 0 minutes | Serves: 6
½ cup rolled oats
2 tbsp peanut butter
1 tbsp honey
1. Mix all ingredients in a bowl.
2. Roll into 6 small balls and refrigerate for 30 minutes.
3. Enjoy one ball as a quick, energy-boosting snack.
Per Serving: Calories 100; Fat 4g; Sodium 20mg; Carbs 12g; Fiber 1g; Sugar 6g; Protein 3g
These snacks are perfect for refueling after a workout while staying within your 1200-calorie limit. Enjoy!

Bonus 5: Expert Q&A: Your Top Questions Answered

To address common concerns and provide expert guidance, this bonus features a comprehensive Q&A with nutritionists and fitness experts. Topics include:

1. Is 1200 calories enough for adults?
Yes, for weight loss under medical supervision, 1200 calories can be safe. However, it's crucial to prioritize nutrient-dense foods to meet your body's needs.

2. Will I feel hungry all the time?
Not if you choose high-fiber, protein-rich foods like vegetables, lean proteins, and whole grains. Staying hydrated also helps curb hunger.

3. Can I exercise on this diet?
Yes, but focus on low-impact activities like walking or yoga. Avoid overexertion, and refuel with a 100-calorie snack post-workout.

4. What if I hit a plateau?
Plateaus are normal. Adjust your calorie intake slightly or vary your exercise routine. Consult a professional if needed.

5. Is "starvation mode" real?
Not at 1200 calories. Starvation mode occurs with extreme, prolonged calorie restriction. This plan is designed for short-term weight loss.

6. Can I eat out on this diet?
Yes! Choose grilled proteins, salads with light dressing, and steamed veggies. Avoid fried foods and sugary drinks.

7. Do I need supplements?
A daily multivitamin can help fill nutritional gaps, but focus on getting nutrients from whole foods first.

8. How do I transition to maintenance?
Gradually increase calories by 100-200 per week while monitoring your weight. Focus on mindful eating and regular exercise.

This bonus ensures you have access to reliable, science-backed information to make informed decisions about your health.

Why These Bonuses Matter?

The 5 exclusive bonuses included with The Dr. Now 1200-Calorie Diet Plan for Beginners are designed to provide a holistic approach to weight loss. They address common challenges, such as meal planning, exercise, mindful eating, and recovery, while offering expert insights to keep you motivated and informed. Together, these bonuses transform the book from a simple diet plan into a comprehensive lifestyle guide, empowering you to achieve your goals with confidence and ease.

By investing in this book, you're not just getting a collection of recipes—you're gaining a complete toolkit for sustainable weight loss and long-term health. Whether you're a beginner or looking to refine your habits, these bonuses ensure you have everything you need to succeed.

120-Day Meal Plan

Here are beginner Dr. Now 1200-Calorie Diet Plan ideas for 3 and 7 days, which you can repeat to cover the whole month.

Month 1 (Day 1 to 30)

1200-Calorie Diet 3-Day Meal Plan

Day 1:
Breakfast: Cauliflower Raspberry Smoothie
Lunch: Chicken Burgers with Tzatziki Sauce
Snack: Crisp Kale Chips
Dinner: Baked Fish with Tomato and Olive

Day 2:
Breakfast: Delicious Tofu Shakshuka
Lunch: Orange and Berries Salad
Snack: Kiwi Chips
Dinner: Garlic Butter Chicken Breast with Cauliflower Rice

Day 3:
Breakfast: Tofu and Spinach Scramble
Lunch: Rosemary Chicken Drumsticks
Snack: Zucchini Feta Roll-Ups
Dinner: Flavorful Artichokes and Carrots

1200-Calorie Diet 7-Day Meal Plan

Day 1:
Breakfast: Apple Chia Seed Milk
Lunch: Turkey Meatballs
Snack: Spicy Cauliflower
Dinner: Turkey and Wild Rice Casserole

Day 2:
Breakfast: Kale and Cherry Tomato Frittata
Lunch: Garlic Cauliflower Mash
Snack: Turkey Spinach Pinwheels
Dinner: Lemony Salmon with Tomatoes and Olives

Day 3:
Breakfast: Classic Shakshuka
Lunch: Chicken and Apple Salad
Snack: Mini Crab Cakes
Dinner: Lemon-Garlic Trout

Day 4:
Breakfast: Stacked Eggplant, Tomato and Egg
Lunch: Roasted Fennel and Cherry Tomatoes
Snack: Garlic Herb Roasted Tomatoes and Olives
Dinner: Greek Chicken Salad

Day 5:
Breakfast: Figs and Tofu Yogurt
Lunch: Homemade Chicken Tagine
Snack: Mini Zucchini & Tomato Frittatas
Dinner: Beef Meatloaf

Day 6:
Breakfast: Turkey & Avocado Breakfast Salad Bowl
Lunch: Delicious Chicken Gyro
Snack: Cucumber Yogurt Dip
Dinner: Beef and Vegetable Stew

Day 7:
Breakfast: Greek Yogurt and Berries Parfait
Lunch: Tuna and Zucchini Burgers
Snack: Edamame & Purple Cabbage Salad
Dinner: Air Fryer Rotisserie Chicken

Month 2 (Day 31 to 60)

1200-Calorie Diet 3-Day Meal Plan

Day 1:
Breakfast: Smoked Salmon and Egg Scramble
Lunch: Artichoke Hearts and Chickpeas Salad
Snack: Greek Yogurt Deviled Eggs
Dinner: Lemon Herb Baked Cod

Day 2:
Breakfast: Poached Eggs with Lemon Avocado Purée
Lunch: Orange Sautéed Spinach
Snack: Lemon White Bean Dip
Dinner: Orange Shrimp Salad

Day 3:
Breakfast: Avocado Egg Boats
Lunch: Chicken Veggie Kebab
Snack: Mint Grapefruit Salad
Dinner: Turkey and Kale Soup

1200-Calorie Diet 7-Day Meal Plan

Day 1:
Breakfast: Berries Oatmeal Muesli
Lunch: Chicken and Quinoa Salad
Snack: Kiwi Chips
Dinner: Lemon Roasted Sea Bass with Root Vegetables

Day 2:
Breakfast: Delicious Tofu Shakshuka
Lunch: Crispy Artichoke Hearts
Snack: Edamame & Purple Cabbage Salad
Dinner: Pan-Seared Scallops with Orange Spinach

Day 3:
Breakfast: Red Pepper and Feta Frittata
Lunch: Rosemary-Roasted Tofu
Snack: Sea Salt Beet Chips
Dinner: Lemon Shrimp Skewers

Day 4:
Breakfast: Greek Yogurt and Berries Parfait
Lunch: Kale and Tuna Bowl
Snack: Spicy Roasted Chickpeas
Dinner: Greek Spiced Chicken

Day 5:
Breakfast: Orange Carrot Smoothie
Lunch: Turkey and Wild Rice Casserole
Snack: Shrimp and Dill Cucumber Bites
Dinner: Baked Parmesan Crusted Tilapia

Day 6:
Breakfast: Mushroom & Spinach Egg Cups
Lunch: Turkey Lettuce Wraps
Snack: Garlic Cauliflower Puree
Dinner: Spicy Halibut with Olives and Tomatoes

Day 7:
Breakfast: Spinach and Egg White Breakfast Wrap
Lunch: Chicken, Broccoli & Peppers Bake
Snack: Roasted Red Pepper and Red Lentil Dip
Dinner: Beef and Zucchini Stew

Month 3 (Day 61 to 90)

1200-Calorie Diet 3-Day Meal Plan

Day 1:
Breakfast: Tofu and Spinach Scramble
Lunch: Vegetable-Barley Salad
Snack: Cucumber Yogurt Dip
Dinner: Smoked Salmon on Cucumber Disks

Day 2:
Breakfast: Figs and Tofu Yogurt
Lunch: Turkey & Butternut Squash Ragout
Snack: Garlic Herb Roasted Tomatoes and Olives
Dinner: Simple Egg Drop Soup

Day 3:
Breakfast: Turkey & Avocado Breakfast Salad Bowl
Lunch: Roasted Zucchini and Bell Peppers
Snack: Mini Zucchini & Tomato Frittatas
Dinner: Turkey, Cauliflower and Kale Soup

1200-Calorie Diet 7-Day Meal Plan

Day 1:
Breakfast: Kale and Cherry Tomato Frittata
Lunch: Asparagus and Strawberry Salad
Snack: Mini Crab Cakes
Dinner: Savory Shredded Beef

Day 2:
Breakfast: Apple Chia Seed Milk
Lunch: Chicken, Broccoli & Peppers Bake
Snack: Kiwi Chips
Dinner: Grilled Lemon Mahi Mahi

Day 3:
Breakfast: Stacked Eggplant, Tomato and Egg
Lunch: Feta & Sun-Dried Tomato Stuffed Chicken Breasts
Snack: Shrimp and Dill Cucumber Bites
Dinner: Garlic Beef and Cauliflower

Day 4:
Breakfast: Cauliflower Raspberry Smoothie
Lunch: Baked Parmesan Chicken Tenders
Snack: Crisp Kale Chips
Dinner: Dill Roasted Whole Red Snapper

Day 5:
Breakfast: Berries Oatmeal Muesli
Lunch: Lemon Herb Chicken Breast
Snack: Zucchini Feta Roll-Ups
Dinner: Easy Beef Burgers

Day 6:
Breakfast: Classic Shakshuka
Lunch: Garlic Butter Chicken Breast with Cauliflower Rice
Snack: Spicy Cauliflower
Dinner: Roasted Salmon with Lemon Zest & Parsley

Day 7:
Breakfast: Spinach and Egg White Breakfast Wrap
Lunch: Spicy Grilled Chicken Thighs
Snack: Spicy Roasted Chickpeas
Dinner: Beef & Brown Rice Stuffed Cabbage Rolls

Month 4 (Day 91 to 120)

1200-Calorie Diet 3-Day Meal Plan

Day 1:
Breakfast: Poached Eggs with Lemon Avocado Purée
Lunch: Grilled Zucchini with Yogurt & Pomegranate Seeds
Snack: Roasted Red Pepper and Red Lentil Dip
Dinner: Shrimp Puttanesca

Day 2:
Breakfast: Berries Oatmeal Muesli
Lunch: Turkey, Cauliflower and Kale Soup
Snack: Greek Yogurt Deviled Eggs
Dinner: Cajun Salmon Po'boy

Day 3:
Breakfast: Avocado Egg Boats
Lunch: Garlic Roasted Grape Tomatoes and Asparagus
Snack: Sea Salt Beet Chips
Dinner: Slow-Cooked Pork Loin and Apple

1200-Calorie Diet 7-Day Meal Plan

Day 1:
Breakfast: Mushroom & Spinach Egg Cups
Lunch: Cabbage Slaw
Snack: Garlic Cauliflower Puree
Dinner: Lemony Salmon with Tomatoes and Olives

Day 2:
Breakfast: Stacked Eggplant, Tomato and Egg
Lunch: Garlic-Herb Roasted Veggies
Snack: Spicy Roasted Chickpeas
Dinner: Chicken and Quinoa Salad

Day 3:
Breakfast: Red Pepper and Feta Frittata
Lunch: Thyme Roasted Butternut Squash with Parmesan
Snack: Mini Crab Cakes
Dinner: Beef, Mushroom and Cabbage Soup

Day 4:
Breakfast: Orange Carrot Smoothie
Lunch: Butternut Squash and Carrot Salad
Snack: Mini Zucchini & Tomato Frittatas
Dinner: Shrimp, Zucchini and Asparagus Stir-Fry

Day 5:
Breakfast: Smoked Salmon and Egg Scramble
Lunch: Sea Salt Roasted Radishes
Snack: Mint Grapefruit Salad
Dinner: Pork Tenderloin and Asparagus Stir-Fry

Day 6:
Breakfast: Greek Yogurt and Berries Parfait
Lunch: Chicken and Vegetable Salad
Snack: Shrimp and Dill Cucumber Bites
Dinner: Salmon and Blueberry Salad

Day 7:
Breakfast: Spinach and Egg White Breakfast Wrap
Lunch: Greek Spiced Chicken
Snack: Turkey Spinach Pinwheels
Dinner: Citrus Kale Salad

Kale and Cherry Tomato Frittata

Prep Time: 10 minutes | Cook Time: 20 minutes | Serves: 4

8 eggs
½ cup unsweetened nondairy milk
½ teaspoon sea salt
½ teaspoon freshly ground black pepper
1 tablespoon extra-virgin olive oil
2 cups kale leaves, chopped
1 red bell pepper, seeded and chopped
1 cup cherry tomatoes, halved

1. Preheat the oven to 400°F.
2. In a large mixing bowl, whisk together the eggs, milk, salt, and black pepper. Set aside.
3. In an oven-safe skillet, warm the olive oil over medium heat. Add the kale, bell pepper, and tomatoes. Cook for about 5 minutes, or until the kale is wilted and bright green.
4. Pour the whisked egg mixture into the skillet and let the eggs begin to set for 30 seconds before gently stirring with a spatula to evenly distribute the vegetables in the eggs.
5. Transfer the skillet to the oven and bake for 12 to 15 minutes, or until the eggs have set.
6. Remove the skillet from the oven and let sit for 5 minutes before serving.
Per Serving: Calories: 190; Total fat: 13g; Saturated fat: 3g; Sodium: 432mg; Carbohydrates: 5g; Fiber: 2g; Sugar: 3g; Protein: 12g

Stacked Eggplant, Tomato and Egg

Prep Time: 15 minutes | Cook Time: 10 minutes | Serves: 4

2 large fresh eggs, whole
1 cup water, for poaching
4 large fresh basil leaves, rinsed, pat-dried
1 piece large green/unripe tomato, sliced into ⅛-inch thick medallions, 4 slices
½ piece large eggplant, sliced into ⅛-inch thick medallions, 4 slices
Olive oil, for frying
Sea salt and white pepper to taste

1. Lightly grease a non-stick skillet with oil, and set this over medium heat. Fry tomato slices until seared on both sides. Transfer cooked pieces to a plate. Do the same for the eggplant slices. Sprinkle cooked pieces with salt and pepper. Set aside.
2. Pour water into a non-stick skillet set over high heat. Bring water to a rolling boil.
3. Carefully crack eggs, and try to keep the yolks whole. Poach eggs until yolks turn milky white but still wobbly. Using a slotted spoon, remove the eggs from the hot water and set them aside.
4. Stack salad in this order: 1 slice of eggplant, 1 slice of tomato, 1 basil leaf, 1 slice of eggplant, 1 slice of tomato, 1 basil leaf, and finally 1 poached egg. Do the same for remaining ingredients.
5. Serve immediately.
Per Serving: Calories 65; Fat 3.66g; Sodium 214mg; Carbs 4.61g; Fiber 2g; Sugar 2.83g; Protein 3.95g

Figs and Tofu Yogurt

Prep Time: 10 minutes | Serves: 4

14 ounces of tofu, silken or soft
1 banana
¼ cup unsweetened nondairy milk
¼ cup freshly squeezed lemon juice
½ cup maple syrup, divided
4 tablespoons ground flaxseed
12 figs, thinly sliced

1. To make the yogurt: In a blender, mix the tofu, banana, milk, lemon juice, and ¼ cup of maple syrup until smooth.
2. Divide the yogurt between 4 bowls. Add 1 tablespoon flaxseed to each bowl and mix.
3. Evenly top each bowl with the fig slices. To finish, drizzle each bowl with the remaining ¼ cup of maple syrup on top.
Per Serving: Calories: 332; Total fat: 6g; Saturated fat: <1g; Sodium: 23mg; Carbohydrates: 68g; Fiber: 7g; Sugar: 54g; Protein: 8g

Orange Carrot Smoothie

Prep Time: 10 minutes | Serves: 2

1 cup 1% low-fat milk
½ cup plain nonfat Greek yogurt
1 medium orange, peeled and sectioned
1 medium banana, sliced and frozen
1 medium carrot, coarsely chopped
1 teaspoon vanilla extract
2 teaspoons grated orange zest

1. Put the milk, yogurt, banana, orange, carrot, vanilla, and orange zest into a high-powered blender. Blend for 30 to 60 seconds or until smooth.
2. Pour into two glasses. Serve immediately.
Per Serving: Calories: 190; Total fat: 2g; Saturated fat: 1g; Sodium: 97mg; Carbohydrates: 34g; Sugar: 23g; Fiber: 4g; Protein: 11g

Red Pepper and Feta Frittata

Prep Time: 10 minutes | Cook Time: 20 minutes | Serves: 4

Olive oil cooking spray
8 large eggs
1 medium red bell pepper, diced
½ teaspoon salt
½ teaspoon black pepper
1 garlic clove, minced
½ cup feta, divided

1. Preheat the air fryer to 360°F. Lightly coat the inside of a 6-inch round cake pan with olive oil cooking spray.
2. In a large bowl, beat the eggs for 1 to 2 minutes, or until well combined.
3. Add the bell pepper, salt, black pepper, and garlic to the eggs, and mix together until the bell pepper is distributed throughout.
4. Fold in ¼ cup of the feta cheese.
5. Pour the egg mixture into the prepared cake pan, and sprinkle the remaining ¼ cup of feta over the top.
6. Place into the air fryer and bake for 18 to 20 minutes, or until the eggs are set in the center.
7. Remove from the air fryer and allow to cool for 5 minutes before serving.
Per Serving: Calories: 204; Total Fat: 14g; Saturated Fat: 6g; Protein: 16g; Total Carbohydrates: 4g; Fiber: 1g; Sugar: 2g; Cholesterol: 389mg

Mushroom & Spinach Egg Cups

Prep Time: 5 minutes | Cook Time: 15 minutes | Serves: 6

Olive oil cooking spray
6 large eggs
1 garlic clove, minced
½ teaspoon salt
½ teaspoon black pepper
Pinch red pepper flakes
8 ounces baby bella mushrooms, sliced
1 cup fresh baby spinach
2 scallions, white parts and green parts, diced

1. Preheat the air fryer to 320°F. Lightly coat the inside of six silicone muffin cups or a six-cup muffin tin with olive oil cooking spray.
2. In a large bowl, beat the eggs, garlic, salt, pepper, and red pepper flakes for 1 to 2 minutes, or until well combined.
3. Fold in the mushrooms, spinach, and scallions.
4. Spoon the mixture equally into each muffin cup.
5. Place into the air fryer and bake for 12 to 15 minutes, or until the eggs are set.
6. Remove and allow to cool for 5 minutes before serving.
Per Serving: Calories: 83; Total Fat: 5g; Saturated Fat: 2g; Protein: 8g; Total Carbohydrates: 2g; Fiber: 1g; Sugar: 1g; Cholesterol: 186mg

Smoked Salmon and Egg Scramble

Prep Time: 10 minutes | Cook Time: 10 minutes | Serves: 4

4 eggs
6 egg whites
⅛ teaspoon freshly ground black pepper
1 tablespoon extra-virgin olive oil
½ red onion, finely chopped
4 ounces smoked salmon, flaked
2 tablespoons capers, drained

1. In a small bowl, whisk the eggs, egg whites, and black pepper. Set aside.
2. In a large nonstick skillet over medium-high heat, heat the olive oil until it shimmers.
3. Add the red onion and cook for about 3 minutes, stirring occasionally, until soft.
4. Add the salmon and capers and cook for 1 minute.
5. Pour the egg mixture into the pan and cook for 3 to 5 minutes, stirring often, until the eggs are fully set.
Per Serving: Calories 152; Fat 7.85g; Sodium 399mg; Carbs 2.22g; Fiber 0.4g; Sugar 1.12g; Protein 17.04g

Avocado Egg Boats

Prep Time: 10 minutes | Cook Time: 8 minutes | Serves: 4

2 avocados, medium-sized
4 eggs, small
1 tsp. dried parsley
1 tsp. salt
1 tsp. pepper

1. Slice each avocado in half, removing the center pit. Season the insides with salt, pepper, and parsley.
2. Crack each egg into the center portion of the avocado. Then place each avocado into the air fryer.
3. Cook the avocado boats in the air fryer for 8 minutes at 325°F.
4. Remove the avocado boats from the air fryer and serve warm with additional salt and black pepper.
Per Serving: Calories 169; Fat 14.11g; Sodium 641mg; Carbs 6.54g; Fiber 4.8g; Sugar 0.35g; Protein 6.17g

Poached Eggs with Lemon Avocado Purée

Prep Time: 15 minutes | Cook Time: 5 minutes | Serves: 4

2 avocados, peeled and pitted
¼ cup chopped fresh basil leaves
3 tablespoons red wine vinegar, divided
Juice of 1 lemon
Zest of 1 lemon
1 garlic clove, minced
1 teaspoon sea salt, divided
⅛ teaspoon freshly ground black pepper
Pinch cayenne pepper, plus more as needed
4 eggs

1. In a blender, blend the avocados, basil, 2 tablespoons of vinegar, garlic, lemon juice and zest, ½ teaspoon of sea salt, pepper, and cayenne until smooth, about 1 minute.
2. Fill a 12-inch nonstick skillet with water, about three-fourths full, and heat over medium. Add the remaining tablespoon of vinegar and ½ teaspoon of sea salt. Bring to a simmer.
3. Gently crack the eggs into custard cups. Carefully lower the cups just above the simmering water, slipping the eggs in one at a time. Turn off the heat, cover the skillet, and let the eggs sit for 5 minutes without disturbing.
4. Use a slotted spoon to gently lift the eggs from the water, letting them drain thoroughly. Place each egg on a plate and spoon the avocado purée over the eggs.

Per Serving: Calories: 213; Protein: 2g; Total Carbohydrates: 11g; Sugars: <1g; Fiber: 7g; Total Fat: 20g; Saturated Fat: 4g; Cholesterol: 0mg; Sodium: 475mg

Delicious Tofu Shakshuka

Prep Time: 15 minutes | Cook Time: 25 minutes | Serves: 4

14 ounces extra-firm tofu, divided
¼ cup water
1 red bell pepper, seeded and chopped
2 teaspoons ground paprika
1 teaspoon ground cumin
1 teaspoon ground coriander
2½ cups canned, diced fire-roasted tomatoes
¾ cup finely chopped fresh parsley, divided
1 avocado, peeled, seeded, and sliced

1. Preheat the oven to 375°F.
2. Take the tofu out of the package and wrap it in a clean cloth or paper towel. Place the tofu on a plate and add a second plate on top. Apply a few heavy cans to the top plate and leave the tofu to "press" for 5 minutes.
3. Evenly slice ¾ of the tofu. Crumble the remaining quarter and set both aside, separately.
4. In an oven-safe skillet with a lid over medium-high heat, sauté the bell pepper for 3 to 4 minutes, until slightly tender.
5. Add the paprika, cumin, and coriander and stir for 1 minute. Stir in the tomatoes and ½ cup of parsley.
6. Place the tofu slices on top, cover the pan with the lid, and let it simmer for 10 minutes.
7. Afterward, remove the lid and transfer the pan to the oven. Bake uncovered for approximately 10 minutes, or until the tofu becomes crisp.
8. Top with the crumbled tofu, remaining ¼ cup parsley, and sliced avocado.
9. Divide between 4 bowls and enjoy.

Per Serving: Calories: 205; Total fat: 10g; Saturated fat: 1g; Sodium: 393mg; Carbohydrates: 16g; Fiber: 7g; Sugar: 6g; Protein: 12g

Berries Oatmeal Muesli

Prep Time: 15 minutes | Cook Time: 20 minutes | Serves: 6

2¾ cups old-fashioned oats or rolled barley
½ cup sliced almonds
2 containers (6 oz each) banana crème or French vanilla fat-free yogurt
1½ cups skim milk
¼ cup ground flaxseed or flaxseed meal
½ cup fresh blueberries
½ cup fresh raspberries
½ cup sliced fresh strawberries

1. Preheat the oven to 350°F. On a baking sheet, spread out the oats and almonds. Bake for 18 to 20 minutes, stirring occasionally, until they turn a light golden brown. Let cool for 15 minutes.
2. In a large bowl, combine the yogurt and milk, mixing until smooth. Stir in oats, almonds and flaxseed.
3. Divide muesli evenly among 6 bowls. Top each serving with berries.
Per Serving: Calories 320; Total Fat 10g (Saturated Fat 2g; Trans Fat 0g); Cholesterol 5mg; Sodium 65mg; Total Carbohydrate 46g (Dietary Fiber 7g; Sugars 15g); Protein 11g

Cauliflower Raspberry Smoothie

Prep Time: 10 minutes | Serves: 2

1 cup frozen cauliflower
1 cup frozen raspberries
Juice of 1 lemon
¼ cup hemp hearts
1 tablespoon chia seeds
1 teaspoon vanilla extract
1½ cups unsweetened nondairy milk

1. In a powerful blender, combine the cauliflower, raspberries, lemon juice, hemp hearts, chia seeds, vanilla, and milk.
2. Blend until smooth.
3. Drink as soon as possible.
Per Serving: Calories 186; Fat 6.48g; Sodium 107mg; Carbs 14.7g; Fiber 9.9g; Sugar 3.75g; Protein 8g

Turkey & Avocado Breakfast Salad Bowl

Prep Time: 10 minutes | Serves: 1

2 slices low-sodium turkey breast
¼ avocado, mashed
1 hard-boiled egg, peeled and sliced
½ cup cherry tomatoes, halved
½ cup cucumber slices
1 teaspoon lemon juice
Salt and pepper, to taste

1. In a small bowl, mash the avocado and season with lemon juice, salt, and pepper.
2. Arrange turkey slices, hard-boiled egg, cherry tomatoes, and cucumber slices in a bowl.
3. Add the mashed avocado to the bowl and serve immediately.
Per Serving: Calories 150; Fat 8g; Sodium 180mg; Carbs 6g; Fiber 3g; Sugar 2g; Protein 15g

Tofu and Spinach Scramble

Prep Time: 10 minutes | Cook Time: 10 minutes | Serves: 4

14 ounces extra-firm tofu
1 tablespoon extra-virgin olive oil
1 white onion, diced
2 garlic cloves, minced
1 red bell pepper, seeded and chopped
1 orange bell pepper, seeded and chopped
2 cups chopped baby spinach
¼ cup nutritional yeast
1 teaspoon turmeric
Sea salt
Freshly ground black pepper
¼ teaspoon black salt (optional)

1. Remove the tofu from the package and wrap in a clean cloth or paper towels. Place the tofu on a plate and add a second plate on top. Apply a few heavy cans to the top plate and leave the tofu to "press" for 5 minutes.
2. Unwrap the tofu and mash in a large bowl with the back of a fork until it's broken into small chunks—like scrambled eggs.
3. In a large nonstick skillet, heat the olive oil. Add the onion, garlic, and red and orange bell peppers and sauté for 4 to 5 minutes, until the onion is translucent.
4. Add the tofu, spinach, nutritional yeast, and turmeric. Cook, stirring occasionally, until the spinach is wilted and the tofu is thoroughly heated.
5. Season with sea salt, black pepper, and the black salt (if using). Divide between 4 plates and serve.
Per Serving: Calories: 188; Total fat: 9g; Saturated fat: 1g; Sodium: 24mg; Carbohydrates: 13g; Fiber: 5g; Sugar: 4g; Protein: 15g

Classic Shakshuka

Prep Time: 15 minutes | Cook Time: 25 minutes | Serves: 4

1 tablespoon extra-virgin olive oil
1 onion, diced
2 tablespoons tomato paste
2 red bell peppers, diced
2 tablespoons Harissa (optional)
4 garlic cloves, minced
2 teaspoons ground cumin
½ teaspoon ground coriander (optional)
1 teaspoon smoked paprika
2 (14-ounce) cans diced tomatoes
4 large eggs
½ cup unsweetened fat-free Greek yogurt

1. Heat the extra-virgin olive oil in a Dutch oven or large saucepan over medium heat. Once the oil starts to shimmer, add the onion and cook for about 3 minutes until translucent.
2. Add the tomato paste, peppers, harissa (if using), garlic, cumin, coriander (if using), paprika, and tomatoes. Bring the mixture to a simmer and cook for 10 to 15 minutes, or until the peppers are tender and the sauce has thickened. Adjust the seasoning as desired.
3. Make four wells in the mixture with the back of a large spoon and gently break one egg into each well. Cover the saucepan and simmer gently for 5 to 8 minutes, or until the egg whites are fully set but the yolks remain runny.
4. Remove the saucepan from the heat and spoon the tomato mixture and one cooked egg into each of four bowls. Top with the Greek yogurt and serve.
Per Serving: Calories 165; Fat 8.93g; Sodium 265mg; Carbs 16.88g; Fiber 5.5g; Sugar 9.98g; Protein 7.17g

Spinach and Egg White Breakfast Wrap

Prep Time: 10 minutes | Cook Time: 5 minutes | Serves: 1

3 egg whites
1 cup fresh spinach
1 low-carb whole wheat tortilla (about 80 calories)
1 tablespoon diced red bell pepper
1 teaspoon chopped chives
1 spray olive oil (for cooking)
Salt and pepper (to taste)

1. Lightly spray a nonstick skillet with olive oil and heat over medium heat.
2. Add spinach and red bell pepper, sautéing until spinach wilts (about 2 minutes).
3. Pour in egg whites, season with salt and pepper, and scramble until fully cooked.
4. Warm the tortilla in the microwave for 10 seconds, then fill with the egg mixture. Sprinkle with chives and roll into a wrap.
Per Serving: Calories 120; Fat 2.5g; Sodium 220mg; Carbs 10g; Fiber 5g; Sugar 1g; Protein 15g

Greek Yogurt and Berries Parfait

Prep Time: 5 minutes | Serves: 1

½ cup fat-free Greek yogurt (about 120g)
¼ cup fresh blueberries
¼ cup fresh strawberries (sliced)
1 tablespoon chia seeds
1 teaspoon sugar-free vanilla syrup (optional)

1. In a small bowl or glass, layer half of the Greek yogurt.
2. Add half of the berries and ½ tablespoon chia seeds.
3. Repeat with the remaining yogurt, berries, and chia seeds. Drizzle with sugar-free vanilla syrup if desired.
Per Serving: Calories 110; Fat 1.5g; Sodium 40mg; Carbs 12g; Fiber 4g; Sugar 6g; Protein 12g

Apple Chia Seed Milk

Prep Time: 10 minutes | Serves: 1

3 tablespoons chia seeds
¾ cup unsweetened nondairy milk
¼ teaspoon ground cinnamon
1 apple, cored and diced

1. In a cereal bowl, mix the chia seeds and milk and let sit for 10 minutes.
2. Add the cinnamon and apple to the chia seed and milk mixture, stir together and enjoy.
Per Serving: Calories 276; Fat 13.1g; Sodium 97mg; Carbs 37.5g; Fiber 16.8g; Sugar 16g; Protein 7.15g

Asparagus and Strawberry Salad

Prep Time: 10 minutes | Cook Time: 12 minutes | Serves: 4

1 lb fresh asparagus spears
Cooking spray
2 tablespoons chopped pecans
1 cup sliced fresh strawberries
4 cups mixed salad greens
¼ cup fat-free balsamic vinaigrette dressing
Cracked pepper, if desired

1. Heat oven to 400°F. Line 15x10x1-inch pan with foil; spray with cooking spray. Trim the tough ends of the asparagus where the stalks naturally snap, then cut them into 1-inch pieces.
2. Place asparagus in single layer in pan; spray with cooking spray. Place pecans in another shallow pan.
3. Bake pecans 5 to 6 minutes or until golden brown, stirring occasionally. Bake asparagus 10 to 12 minutes or until crisp-tender. Cool pecans and asparagus 8 to 10 minutes or until room temperature.
4. In medium bowl, mix asparagus, pecans, strawberries, greens and dressing. Sprinkle with pepper.
Per Serving: Calories 90; Total Fat 3g (Saturated Fat 0g; Trans Fat 0g); Cholesterol 0mg; Sodium 180mg; Total Carbohydrate 11g (Dietary Fiber 4g; Sugars 6g); Protein 4g

Grilled Zucchini with Yogurt & Pomegranate Seeds

Prep Time: 10 minutes | Cook Time: 6 minutes | Serves: 4

4 zucchinis, sliced
2 tablespoons extra-virgin olive oil
¾ teaspoon sea salt, divided
¼ cup unsweetened nonfat plain Greek yogurt
1 teaspoon chili powder
¼ cup pomegranate seeds

1. Preheat the grill to high heat.
2. Brush the zucchini pieces on both sides with olive oil and sprinkle with ½ teaspoon of sea salt. Grill for about 3 minutes per side until soft and starting to brown. Arrange on a platter.
3. In a small bowl, whisk the yogurt, chili powder, and remaining ¼ teaspoon of sea salt. Drizzle over the zucchini. Sprinkle with the pomegranate seeds.
Per Serving: Calories: 154; Protein: 8g; Total Carbohydrates: 20g; Sugars: 11g; Fiber: 3g; Total Fat: 8g; Saturated Fat: 1g; Cholesterol: 1mg; Sodium: 388mg

Cabbage Slaw

Prep Time: 20 minutes | Serves: 2

100g (3½oz) carrots, scrubbed and coarsely grated
200g (7oz) red or white cabbage
240g (8½oz) cooked or canned chickpeas, black, borlotti or cannellini beans, drained
1 green chili or a pinch of chili flakes
a small handful of coriander or flat-leaf parsley, roughly chopped
1 tablespoon extra-virgin olive oil
juice of ½ lemon or a splash of cider vinegar
½ teaspoon ground cumin
½ teaspoon black onion (nigella) seeds
For the Tahini Dressing:
2 tablespoons tahini
juice of ½ lemon or a splash of cider vinegar
salt and freshly ground black pepper
To serve (optional):
4 soft-boiled eggs, halved
1 teaspoon sesame seeds
A handful of toasted nuts, such as hazelnuts, almonds or peanuts, chopped

1. Combine the dressing ingredients, then incorporate 2 tablespoons of water to achieve a smooth, creamy texture. Adjust the flavor to your preference by adding more lemon juice, salt, and pepper as needed. Use straight away or keep in the fridge for up to 3 days.
2. Mix all the salad ingredients together in a large bowl. Divide between 2 salad bowls, splash over the dressing and serve.
Per Serving: Calories 259; Fat 6.81g; Sodium 890mg; Carbs 42.35g; Fiber 12g; Sugar 11.74g; Protein 11.03g

Sesame Broccoli

Prep Time: 5 minutes | Cook Time: 15 minutes | Serves: 4

1 tablespoon extra-virgin olive oil
1 tablespoon low-sodium soy sauce
½ tablespoon sesame oil
1 head broccoli
1 tablespoon toasted sesame seeds

1. Preheat the oven to 450°F. Line a baking sheet with parchment paper.
2. In a medium bowl, whisk together the extra-virgin olive oil, soy sauce, and sesame oil. Add the broccoli and toss to evenly coat it.
3. Place the coated broccoli on the prepared baking sheet and bake for 10 minutes, or until tender.
4. Remove the sheet from the oven, flip the broccoli, and return it to bake for another 5 to 10 minutes.
5. Serve the broccoli with toasted sesame seeds on top.
6. Store any leftovers in an airtight container in the refrigerator for up to 4 days.
Per Serving: Calories: 110; Total fat: 7g; Carbohydrates: 11g; Fiber: 4g; Protein: 5g; Calcium: 75mg; Vitamin D: 0mcg; Vitamin B12: 0mcg; Iron: 1mg; Zinc: 1mg

Crispy Artichoke Hearts

Prep Time: 10 minutes | Cook Time: 15 minutes | Serves: 2

1 (15-ounce) can artichoke hearts in water, drained
1 egg
1 tablespoon water
¼ cup whole wheat bread crumbs
¼ teaspoon salt
¼ teaspoon paprika
½ lemon

1. Preheat the air fryer to 380°F.
2. In a medium shallow bowl, whisk the egg and water until frothy.
3. In a separate medium shallow bowl, mix together the bread crumbs, salt, and paprika.
4. Dip each artichoke heart into the egg mixture, then coat with the bread crumb mixture, ensuring the outside is fully covered. Place the artichokes hearts in a single layer of the air fryer basket.
5. Fry the artichoke hearts for 15 minutes.
6. Remove the artichokes from the air fryer and squeeze fresh lemon juice over them before serving.
Per Serving: Calories: 91; Total Fat: 2g; Saturated Fat: 1g; Protein: 5g; Total Carbohydrates: 16g; Fiber: 8g; Sugar: 1g; Cholesterol: 47mg

Orange and Berries Salad

Prep Time: 15 minutes | Serves: 8

¼ cup fat-free or reduced-fat mayonnaise
3 tablespoons sugar
1 tablespoon white vinegar
2 teaspoons poppy seed
2 cups fresh strawberry halves
2 cups fresh blueberries
1 orange, peeled, chopped
Sliced almonds, if desired

1. In a small bowl, mix mayonnaise, sugar, vinegar and poppy seed with whisk until well blended.
2. In a medium bowl, mix strawberries, blueberries and orange. Right before serving, drizzle the dressing over the fruit and gently toss to coat. Sprinkle with almonds.
Per Serving: Calories 70; Total Fat 1g (Saturated Fat 0g; Trans Fat 0g); Cholesterol 0mg; Sodium 60mg; Total Carbohydrate 16g (Dietary Fiber 2g; Sugars 12g); Protein 0g

Sea Salt Roasted Radishes

Prep Time: 5 minutes | Cook Time: 18 minutes | Serves: 4

1 pound radishes, ends trimmed if needed
2 tablespoons olive oil
½ teaspoon sea salt

1. Preheat the air fryer to 360°F.
2. In a large bowl, combine the radishes with olive oil and sea salt.
3. Pour the radishes into the air fryer and cook for 10 minutes. Stir or turn the radishes over and cook for 8 minutes more, then serve.
Per Serving: Calories: 78; Total Fat: 9g; Saturated Fat: 1g; Protein: 1g; Total Carbohydrates: 4g; Fiber: 2g; Sugar: 2g; Cholesterol: 0mg

Rosemary-Roasted Tofu

Prep Time: 15 minutes | Cook Time: 25 minutes | Serves: 4

14 ounces extra-firm tofu
1 tablespoon extra-virgin olive oil
1 tablespoon low-sodium soy sauce
½ teaspoon garlic powder
1 teaspoon finely chopped dried rosemary
2 tablespoons cornstarch, divided

1. Remove the tofu from the package and wrap in a clean cloth or paper towels. Place the tofu on a plate and add a second plate on top. Weigh down the top plate with a few heavy cans and leave the tofu to "press" for 5 minutes.
2. Preheat the oven to 400°F.
3. In a medium mixing bowl, whisk together the olive oil, soy sauce, garlic powder, rosemary, and 1 tablespoon of cornstarch until smooth.
4. Cut the tofu block in half lengthwise and then cut each rectangle into about 16 pieces.
5. Toss the tofu in the sauce and stir well to combine. Add the remaining 1 tablespoon of cornstarch to the mixture and stir until well combined.
6. Place the tofu cubes on a baking sheet in a single layer and bake in the oven for 25 minutes, flipping them halfway through at the 15-minute mark.
Per Serving: Calories: 155; Total fat: 9g; Saturated fat: 1g; Sodium: 226mg; Carbohydrates: 8g; Fiber: 1g; Sugar: 0g; Protein: 11g

Garlic Cauliflower Mash

Prep Time: 10 minutes | Cook Time: 20 minutes | Serves: 4

4 cups cauliflower, raw or frozen defrosted
4 garlic cloves, peeled
2 tablespoons, plus 1 teaspoon extra-virgin olive oil, divided
1 teaspoon dried thyme
¼ teaspoon sea salt
¼ cup unsweetened nondairy milk

1. Preheat the oven to 375°F.
2. Chop the cauliflower into smaller florets.
3. In a large bowl, toss the florets and whole garlic with 2 tablespoons of olive oil, the thyme, and the salt.
4. On a large, rimmed baking sheet, arrange the garlic and cauliflower and roast them in the oven for 20 minutes, stirring after 10 minutes.
5. Remove the roasted vegetables from the oven and put them into a blender with the milk and 1 teaspoon of olive oil.
6. Blend until smooth, or to your desired mashed consistency.
Per Serving: Calories: 104; Total fat: 8g; Saturated fat: 1g; Sodium: 190mg; Carbohydrates: 7g; Fiber: 2g; Sugar: 2g; Protein: 2g

Garlic Roasted Grape Tomatoes and Asparagus

Prep Time: 5 minutes | Cook Time: 12 minutes | Serves: 6

2 cups grape tomatoes
1 bunch asparagus, trimmed
2 tablespoons olive oil
3 garlic cloves, minced
½ teaspoon kosher salt

1. Preheat the air fryer to 380ºF.
2. In a large bowl, combine all of the ingredients, tossing until the vegetables are well coated with oil.
3. Pour the vegetable mixture into the air fryer basket and spread into a single layer, then roast for 12 minutes.
Per Serving: Calories: 57; Total Fat: 5g; Saturated Fat: 1g; Protein: 1g; Total Carbohydrates: 4g; Fiber: 1g; Sugar: 2g; Cholesterol: 0mg

Garlic-Herb Roasted Veggies

Prep Time: 15 minutes | Cook Time: 30 minutes | Serves: 4

1 large sweet potato
2 medium beets
2 medium carrots
1 zucchini
2 tablespoons extra-virgin olive oil
2 tablespoons balsamic vinegar
4 garlic cloves, minced
2 teaspoons dried basil
2 teaspoons dried oregano
2 cups cremini mushrooms
1 red onion, chopped
Sea salt
Freshly ground black pepper

1. Preheat the oven to 425°F.
2. Dice the sweet potato, beets, carrots, and zucchini into ½-inch cubes.
3. In a small bowl, whisk together the olive oil, balsamic vinegar, garlic, basil, and oregano.
4. On a rimmed baking sheet, arrange the diced vegetables, mushrooms, and onion in a single layer. Drizzle the oil mixture over the vegetables, then toss to ensure they are evenly coated. Season with salt and pepper to taste.
5. Roast in the oven for 15 minutes.
6. Stir the vegetables after 15 minutes and continue roasting them for an additional 10 to 15 minutes, or until the vegetables are tender.

Per Serving: Calories: 177; Total fat: 7g; Saturated fat: 1g; Sodium: 92mg; Carbohydrates: 25g; Fiber: 5g; Sugar: 11g; Protein: 5g

Roasted Fennel and Cherry Tomatoes

Prep Time: 10 minutes | Cook Time: 25 minutes | Serves: 4

2 fennel bulbs, cored and cut into ½-inch-thick pieces
20 cherry tomatoes, halved
¼ cup extra-virgin olive oil
½ teaspoon sea salt
¼ teaspoon freshly ground black pepper

1. Preheat the oven to 425°F.
2. In a large bowl, toss the fennel and tomatoes with the olive oil, sea salt, and pepper. Arrange them in a single, even layer on a rimmed baking sheet or in a roasting pan. Roast for 20 to 25 minutes until the fennel is soft and browned.
3. Serve hot.

Per Serving: Calories: 237; Protein: 7g; Total Carbohydrates: 33g; Sugars: 16g; Fiber: 11g; Total Fat: 12g; Saturated Fat: 1g; Cholesterol: 0mg; Sodium: 325mg

Roasted Zucchini and Bell Peppers

Prep Time: 10 minutes | Cook Time: 15 minutes | Serves: 6

2 medium zucchini, cubed
1 red bell pepper, diced
2 garlic cloves, sliced
2 tablespoons olive oil
½ teaspoon salt and black pepper

1. Preheat the air fryer to 380°F.
2. In a large bowl, mix together the bell pepper, zucchini, and garlic with the olive oil and salt.
3. Pour the mixture into the air fryer basket, and roast for 7 minutes. Shake or stir, then roast for 7 to 8 minutes more.

Per Serving: Calories: 60; Total Fat: 5g; Saturated Fat: 1g; Protein: 1g; Total Carbohydrates: 4g; Fiber: 1g; Sugar: 2g; Cholesterol: 0mg

Cauliflower Rice Casserole

Prep Time: 10 minutes | Cook Time: 25 minutes | Serves: 4

2 tablespoons avocado oil
¼ cup diced yellow onion
1 garlic clove, minced
½ cup low-sodium chicken broth
1 tablespoon tomato paste
1 tablespoon taco seasoning
4 cups cauliflower rice
½ red bell pepper, seeded and finely diced
½ cup shredded fat-free Mozzarella cheese

1. Preheat the oven to 375°F.
2. Heat the oil in a medium skillet over medium heat and add the onion. Sauté over medium heat until the onion starts to soften and becomes translucent, about 5 minutes. Add the garlic and cook for 1 minute or until fragrant.
3. Add the chicken broth, tomato paste, and taco seasoning to the skillet. Mix well to combine and bring it to a boil. Reduce the heat to low and simmer for 2 to 3 minutes.
4. Add the cauliflower rice and bell pepper and mix well.
5. Transfer the cauliflower rice mixture to an 8-inch square casserole dish. Top with cheese and bake for about 15 minutes, or until the cheese is melted and bubbly. Serve immediately.
6. Refrigerate leftovers in an airtight container for up to 4 days.
Per Serving: Calories 152; Fat 8.46g; Sodium 452mg; Carbs 11.65g; Fiber 2.8g; Sugar 5.31g; Protein 8.78g

Thyme Roasted Butternut Squash with Parmesan

Prep Time: 15 minutes | Cook Time: 20 minutes | Serves: 4

2½ cups butternut squash, cubed into 1-inch pieces (approximately 1 medium)
2 tablespoons olive oil
¼ teaspoon salt
¼ teaspoon garlic powder
¼ teaspoon black pepper
1 tablespoon fresh thyme
¼ cup grated Parmesan

1. Preheat the air fryer to 360°F.
2. In a large bowl, combine the cubed squash with the olive oil, salt, garlic powder, pepper, and thyme until the squash is well coated.
3. Pour this mixture into the air fryer basket, and roast for 10 minutes. Stir and roast another 8 to 10 minutes more.
4. Remove the squash from the air fryer and toss with freshly grated Parmesan before serving.
Per Serving: Calories: 127; Total Fat: 9g; Saturated Fat: 2g; Protein: 3g; Total Carbohydrates: 11g; Fiber: 2g; Sugar: 2g; Cholesterol: 5mg

Orange Sautéed Spinach

Prep Time: 5 minutes | Cook Time: 5 minutes | Serves: 4

2 tablespoons extra-virgin olive oil
4 cups fresh baby spinach
1 teaspoon orange zest
¼ cup freshly squeezed orange juice
½ teaspoon sea salt
⅛ teaspoon freshly ground black pepper

1. In a large skillet over medium-high heat, heat the olive oil until it shimmers.
2. Add the spinach and orange zest. Cook for about 3 minutes, stirring occasionally, until the spinach wilts.
3. Stir in the orange juice, sea salt, and pepper. Cook for 2 minutes more, stirring occasionally. Serve hot.
Per Serving: Calories: 74; Protein: 7g; Total Carbohydrates: 3g; Sugars: 1g; Fiber: <1g; Total Fat: 7g; Saturated Fat: <1g; Cholesterol: 0mg; Sodium: 258mg

Flavorful Artichokes and Carrots

Prep Time: 15 minutes | Cook Time: 40 minutes | Serves: 4

¼ cup extra-virgin olive oil, divided
1 cup sliced onion
12 whole baby carrots
½ cup chopped celery
Juice of 1 lemon
¾ cup water
10 frozen artichoke hearts, halved
¼ cup chopped fresh dill
½ teaspoon sea salt
⅛ teaspoon freshly ground black pepper
¾ cup peas

1. In a large pot over medium-high heat, heat 2 tablespoons of olive oil until it shimmers.
2. Add the onion, carrots, and celery. Cook for 5 to 10 minutes, stirring occasionally, until the vegetables are tender.
3. Add the lemon juice, water, and the remaining 2 tablespoons of olive oil. Bring to a boil. Reduce the heat to medium-low and simmer for about 15 minutes until the carrots are tender, adding more water as needed.
4. Add the artichoke hearts, dill, sea salt, and pepper. Cover and cook for 10 minutes more until the artichokes are tender.
5. Stir in the peas just before serving.
Per Serving: Calories: 273; Protein: 9g; Total Carbohydrates: 33g; Sugars: 7g; Fiber: 15g; Total Fat: 15g; Saturated Fat: 2g; Cholesterol: 0mg; Sodium: 471mg

Chapter 3 Poultry Recipes

Chicken Burgers with Tzatziki Sauce

Prep Time: 30 minutes | Cook Time: 12 minutes | Serves: 4

Tzatziki Sauce:
1 medium peeled or unpeeled cucumber
½ cup plain Greek yogurt (from 6-oz container)
2 tablespoons chopped onion
2 teaspoons chopped fresh mint
Burgers:
1 lb lean ground chicken
1 cup chopped fresh spinach
¼ cup chopped pitted kalamata olives
1 tablespoon cornstarch
1 tablespoon chopped fresh oregano leaves
2 cloves garlic, chopped
¼ teaspoon salt
¼ teaspoon pepper
2 whole-grain pita breads (6 inch), cut in half
½ cup chopped fresh tomato

1. Set oven control to broil. Chop enough cucumber to equal ½ cup; place in small bowl (cut 12 thin slices from remaining cucumber for sandwiches; set aside). Stir in remaining sauce ingredients; refrigerate until ready to use.
2. In large bowl, mix chicken, spinach, olives, cornstarch, oregano, garlic, salt and pepper. Shape into 4 oval patties, each about ½ inch thick. Place the patties on a broiler pan. Broil with the tops about 5 inches from the heat for 10 to 12 minutes, flipping once, until the internal temperature reaches at least 165°F.
3. Place burgers in pita halves. To serve, top each burger with tomato, cucumber slices and about 3 tablespoons sauce.
Per Serving: Calories 260; Total Fat 8g (Saturated Fat 2g; Trans Fat 0g); Cholesterol 65mg; Sodium 460mg; Total Carbohydrate 25g (Dietary Fiber 3g; Sugars 6g); Protein 20g

Turkey Meatballs

Prep Time: 5 minutes | Cook Time: 12 minutes | Serves: 4

1 pound ground turkey
1 egg
¼ teaspoon red pepper flakes
¼ cup whole wheat bread crumbs
1 teaspoon salt
½ teaspoon garlic powder
½ teaspoon onion powder
½ teaspoon black pepper

1. Preheat the air fryer to 360°F.
2. In a large bowl, combine all of the ingredients and mix well.
3. Separate the meatball mixture into 12 equal portions. Roll each portion into a ball and arrange them in a single layer at the bottom of the air fryer basket, ensuring they are not touching each other.
4. Cook for 10 to 12 minutes, or until the meatballs are cooked through and browned.
Per Serving: Calories: 217; Total Fat: 11g; Saturated Fat: 3g; Protein: 24g; Total Carbohydrates: 5g; Fiber: 0g; Sugar: 0g; Cholesterol: 130mg

Turkey & Butternut Squash Ragout

Prep Time: 15 minutes | Cook Time: 7 to 8 hours | Serves: 4

1½ lb turkey thighs, skin removed
1 small butternut squash (about 2 lb), peeled, seeded, cut into 1½-inch pieces
1 medium onion, cut into slices
1 can (16 oz) baked beans, undrained
1 can (14.5 oz) diced tomatoes with Italian herbs, undrained
2 tablespoons chopped fresh parsley

1. Spray a 3 to 4-quart slow cooker with cooking spray. In slow cooker, mix all ingredients except parsley.
2. Cover; cook on Low heat setting 7 to 8 hours.
3. Transfer turkey from slow cooker to cutting board. Remove meat from bones; discard bones. Return the turkey to slow cooker and stir to reheat. Just before serving, sprinkle with parsley.
Per Serving: Calories 344; Fat 11.17g; Sodium 1723mg; Carbs 28.39g; Fiber 7.3g; Sugar 9.2g; Protein 36.08g

Chicken, Broccoli & Peppers Bake

Prep Time: 10 minutes | Cook Time: 20 minutes | Serves: 4

¼ cup extra-virgin olive oil, divided
¼ cup white wine vinegar
2 teaspoons Dijon mustard
1 teaspoon sea salt, divided
8 cups broccoli, chopped into small florets
4 orange bell peppers, thinly sliced
4 boneless, skinless chicken breasts, sliced into strips

1. Preheat the oven to 375°F.
2. In a large bowl, whisk together 3 tablespoons of olive oil, the vinegar, the mustard, and ½ teaspoon of salt.
3. Gently toss the broccoli and bell pepper slices in the bowl with the olive oil mixture until they are well coated.
4. Spread the vegetables on a rimmed baking sheet.
5. Add the chicken, the remaining 1 tablespoon of olive oil, and ½ teaspoon of salt to the bowl. Mix until the chicken is well coated and then transfer the chicken to the baking sheet with the broccoli and bell peppers.
6. Bake in the oven for 20 minutes, or until the chicken is fully cooked and the vegetables are tender.
Per Serving: Calories: 350; Total fat: 18g; Saturated fat: 3g; Sodium: 760mg; Carbohydrates: 19g; Fiber: 7g; Sugar: 8g; Protein: 31g

Rosemary Chicken Drumsticks

Prep Time: 5 minutes | Cook Time: 1 hour | Serves: 6

2 tablespoons chopped fresh rosemary leaves
1 teaspoon garlic powder
½ teaspoon sea salt
⅛ teaspoon freshly ground black pepper
Zest of 1 lemon
12 chicken drumsticks, skinless

1. Preheat the oven to 350°F.
2. In a small bowl, combine the rosemary, garlic powder, sea salt, pepper, and lemon zest.
3. Place the drumsticks in a 9-by-13-inch baking dish and sprinkle with the rosemary mixture. Bake for about 1 hour, or until the chicken reaches an internal temperature of 165°F.
Per Serving: Calories: 163; Protein: 26g; Total Carbohydrates: 2g; Sugars: <1g; Fiber: <1g; Total Fat: 6g; Saturated Fat: 2g; Cholesterol: 81mg; Sodium: 309mg

Chicken Veggie Kebab

Prep Time: 30 minutes | Cook Time: 25 minutes | Serves: 4

¼ cup olive oil
1 teaspoon garlic powder
1 teaspoon onion powder
1 teaspoon ground cumin
½ teaspoon dried oregano
½ teaspoon dried basil
¼ cup lemon juice
1 tablespoon apple cider vinegar
Olive oil cooking spray
1 pound boneless skinless chicken thighs, cut into 1-inch pieces
1 red bell pepper, cut into 1-inch pieces
1 red onion, cut into 1-inch pieces
1 zucchini, cut into 1-inch pieces
12 cherry tomatoes

1. In a large bowl, mix together the olive oil, onion powder, garlic powder, cumin, basil, oregano, lemon juice, and apple cider vinegar.
2. Spray six skewers with olive oil cooking spray.
3. On each skewer, slide on a piece of chicken, then a piece of bell pepper, onion, zucchini, and finally a tomato and then repeat. Each skewer should have at least two pieces of each item.
4. Once all of the skewers are prepared, place them in a 9-by-13-inch baking dish and pour the olive oil marinade over the top of the skewers. Turn each skewer so that all sides of the chicken and vegetables are coated.
5. Cover the dish with plastic wrap and place it in the refrigerator for 30 minutes.
6. After 30 minutes, preheat the air fryer to 380°F. (If using a grill attachment, make sure it is inside the air fryer during preheating.)
7. Remove the skewers from the marinade and lay them in a single layer in the air fryer basket. If the air fryer has a grill attachment, you can also lay them on this instead.
8. Cook for 10 minutes. Rotate the kebabs, then cook them for 15 minutes more.
9. Remove the skewers from the air fryer and let them rest for 5 minutes before serving.
Per Serving: Calories: 304; Total Fat: 17g; Saturated Fat: 3g; Protein: 27g; Total Carbohydrates: 10g; Fiber: 3g; Sugar: 5g; Cholesterol: 83mg

Greek Spiced Chicken

Prep Time: 10 minutes | Cook Time: 15 minutes | Serves: 4

1 pound boneless skinless chicken breasts, cubed
¼ cup nonfat plain Greek yogurt
2 tablespoons olive oil
1 teaspoon dried oregano
1 teaspoon ground cumin
1 teaspoon ground cinnamon
1 teaspoon salt
¼ teaspoon ground turmeric
¼ teaspoon black pepper
Greek salad, for serving (optional)
Tzatziki sauce, for serving (optional)

1. Preheat the air fryer to 380°F.
2. In a large bowl, combine all ingredients and mix together until the chicken is coated well.
3. Spread the chicken mixture in an even layer in the air fryer basket, then cook for 10 minutes. Stir the chicken mixture and cook for an additional 5 minutes.
4. Serve with a Greek salad, and tzatziki sauce.
Per Serving: Calories: 209; Total Fat: 10g; Saturated Fat: 2g; Protein: 27g; Total Carbohydrates: 2g; Fiber: 0g; Sugar: 1g; Cholesterol: 83mg

Air Fryer Rotisserie Chicken

Prep Time: 10 minutes | Cook Time: 65 minutes | Serves: 6

1 rotisserie chicken, washed and patted dry
1 tsp. parsley, dried
1 tsp. garlic powder
1 tsp. black pepper
1 tsp. salt
2 tbsp. olive oil

1. Remove the giblets from inside the chicken, rinse the chicken thoroughly, and pat it dry with paper towels.
2. Rub the olive oil over the chicken, coating it well. Season the chicken with the spices, rubbing them in well to coat.
3. Place the rotisserie chicken in the air fryer basket, positioning it breast-side down. Cook the chicken in the air fryer for 30 minutes at 350°F.
4. Flip the chicken so that the belly faces up. Cook at 350°F for 35 minutes this time.
5. Check the inside of the chicken with your meat thermometer, making sure it reaches 165°F.
6. Allow the chicken to rest for about 10 to 15 minutes before serving.
Per Serving: Calories 219; Fat 8.81g; Sodium 507mg; Carbs 0.7g; Fiber 0.2g; Sugar 0g; Protein 32.47g

Greek Chicken Salad

Prep Time: 20 minutes | Cook Time: 25 minutes | Serves: 4

1 pound boneless, skinless chicken breasts
¾ cup chopped spinach
½ cup diced celery
½ cup red grapes, quartered
¼ cup chopped pecans
2 tablespoons dried cherries or raisins
½ cup nonfat plain Greek yogurt
½ teaspoon poultry seasoning
¼ teaspoon onion powder
¼ teaspoon freshly ground black pepper
⅛ teaspoon salt

1. Bring a large pot of water to a boil over medium-high heat. Add the chicken and cook for about 25 minutes.
2. Using a slotted spoon, transfer the chicken to a large mixing bowl, reserving ¼ cup of the cooking liquid. Once the chicken is cool enough to handle, cut it into small pieces and add the reserved cooking liquid.
3. Add the remaining ingredients and mix everything together. Enjoy!
Per Serving: Calories 224; Fat 10g; Sodium 347mg; Carbs 10g, Fiber 2g; Sugar 7g; Protein 27g

Turkey and Wild Rice Casserole

Prep Time: 10 minutes | Cook Time: 1 hour 15 minutes | Serves: 6

2 cups cut-up cooked turkey or chicken
2¼ cups boiling water
⅓ cup fat-free (skim) milk
4 medium green onions, sliced (¼ cup)
1 can (10.75 oz) condensed 98% fat-free cream of mushroom soup
1 package (6 oz) original long-grain and wild rice mix
Additional green onions, if desired

1. Heat the oven to 350°F. In ungreased 2-quart casserole, mix all ingredients, including seasoning packet from rice mix.
2. Cover; bake 45 to 50 minutes or until rice is tender. Uncover and bake for an additional 10 to 15 minutes, or until the liquid has been absorbed. Sprinkle with additional green onions.
Per Serving: Calories 220; Total Fat 4.5g (Saturated Fat 1g; Trans Fat 0g); Cholesterol 45mg; Sodium 740mg; Total Carbohydrate 27g (Dietary Fiber 1g; Sugars 2g); Protein 17g

Chicken and Quinoa Salad

Prep Time: 15 minutes | Cook Time: 35 minutes | Serves: 4

4 boneless, skinless chicken breasts (about 1 pound)
¼ cup aged balsamic vinegar
1 tablespoon extra-virgin olive oil
1 teaspoon honey
2 or 3 garlic cloves, minced
½ teaspoon freshly ground black pepper
¾ cup uncooked quinoa
2 cups low-sodium chicken broth
4 cups spinach
Pinch salt, if desired

1. Put the chicken in a zip-top bag.
2. In a small bowl, whisk together the vinegar, oil, honey, garlic, and pepper. Pour half of the mixture into the bag with the chicken, seal it, and toss a few times to make sure the marinade is distributed over all the chicken. Refrigerate for at least 30 minutes. (Reserve the rest of the balsamic mixture for serving.)
3. Preheat the oven to 400°F.
4. Transfer the chicken to an 8-inch square baking dish. Bake until a thermometer inserted in a breast reads 165°F, 30 to 35 minutes.
5. While the chicken is in the oven, combine the quinoa and chicken broth in a small saucepan. Bring to a boil over medium-high heat, then reduce to a simmer, cover, and cook until the liquid is evaporated, about 15 minutes. Five minutes before the quinoa is done, add the spinach.
6. Serve the chicken on top of the quinoa and spinach mixture. Drizzle with the reserved balsamic mixture and a pinch of salt, if desired.
Per Serving: Calories 332; Fat 9.14g; Sodium 291mg; Carbs 27.85g; Fiber 3g; Sugar 4.14g; Protein 33.48g

Crisp Chicken Drumsticks

Prep Time: 15 minutes | Cook Time: 45 minutes | Serves: 4

Nonstick cooking spray
4 chicken drumsticks, skin removed
½ teaspoon onion powder
½ teaspoon garlic powder
½ teaspoon salt
¼ teaspoon freshly ground black pepper
1 large egg
2 tablespoons unsweetened almond milk
¼ cup grated Parmesan cheese
4 tablespoons whole-wheat bread crumbs

1. Preheat the oven to 375°F. Coat a small baking pan with nonstick cooking spray.
2. Season the drumsticks with the onion powder, garlic powder, salt, and pepper.
3. In a shallow bowl, whisk together the egg and almond milk. In another shallow bowl, combine the Parmesan cheese and bread crumbs.
4. One by one, dip each drumstick into the egg mixture. Shake to let the excess drip off. Roll the drumsticks in the bread crumb mixture and place in the baking pan.
5. Bake, turning the drumsticks over halfway through cooking, until the coating is browned and the juices run clear, about 45 minutes.
Per Serving: Calories 190; Fat 5g; Sodium 445mg; Carbs 5g; Fiber 1g; Sugar 1g; Protein 13g

Homemade Chicken Tagine

Prep Time: 15 minutes | Cook Time: 35 minutes | Serves: 6

3 tablespoons olive oil
1 onion, sliced
2 carrots, cut into long ribbons
2 red bell peppers, coarsely chopped
3 garlic cloves, minced
3 pounds boneless, skinless chicken thighs
1 cup chicken broth
1 tablespoon tomato paste
1 teaspoon ground coriander
½ teaspoon ground turmeric
1 to 2 tablespoons harissa
¼ cup chopped dried apricots
Sea salt
Freshly ground black pepper

1. In a large stockpot, heat the olive oil over medium-high heat. Add the onion, carrots, bell peppers, and garlic and sauté for 5 to 7 minutes, until softened. Add the chicken to the pan and cook, turning occasionally to ensure the chicken browns evenly on all sides, for about 7 minutes.
2. In a small bowl, stir together the broth, tomato paste, coriander, turmeric, and harissa until well combined. Add the broth mixture to the stockpot and stir well. Add the apricots and season with salt and pepper.
3. Bring to a boil, reduce the heat to low, cover, and simmer for 20 minutes, or until the chicken is cooked through and has an internal temperature of 165°F. Serve.

Per Serving: Calories 376; Fat 16.4g; Sodium 578mg; Carbs 9.48g; Fiber 1.7g; Sugar 5.81g; Protein 45.97g

Delicious Chicken Gyro

Prep Time: 20 minutes | Cook Time: 10 minutes | Serves: 6

2 tablespoons olive oil
Zest and juice of ½ lemon
1 tablespoon dried oregano
1½ teaspoons dried thyme
1 garlic clove, minced
¼ teaspoon sea salt
¼ teaspoon freshly ground black pepper
2 pounds boneless, skinless chicken thighs, cut into ½-inch-thick strips
6 whole-wheat pita breads
3 Roma (plum) tomatoes, diced
½ red onion, thinly sliced
⅓ cup Tzatziki
⅛ cup crumbled feta cheese

1. In a large bowl, stir together the olive oil, lemon zest, lemon juice, garlic, oregano, thyme, salt, and pepper. Add the chicken and toss to evenly coat. Cover the bowl and marinate in the refrigerator for 30 minutes.
2. Heat a large skillet over medium-high heat. Add the chicken (discard the marinade) and cook for 7 to 10 minutes, until cooked through. Transfer the chicken to a plate.
3. Place the pitas on a clean work surface and top each with 3 or 4 strips of chicken. Evenly divide the tomatoes, onion, tzatziki, and feta among the pitas.
4. Fold the pitas over to enclose the toppings and serve.

Per Serving: Calories 346; Fat 12.34g; Sodium 825mg; Carbs 23.7g; Fiber 3.4g; Sugar 5.9g; Protein 35.15g

Garlic Butter Chicken Breast with Cauliflower Rice

Prep Time: 15 minutes | Cook Time: 15 minutes | Serves: 4

4 tablespoons cold salted butter, divided
1 pound boneless, skinless chicken breast, cut into 1-inch cubes
1 teaspoon kosher salt, divided
¼ teaspoon freshly ground black pepper
2 garlic cloves, minced
½ cup low-sodium chicken broth
3 cups cauliflower rice
¼ cup water
2 tablespoons chopped fresh parsley
¼ teaspoon paprika

1. In a large skillet over medium heat, melt 2 tablespoons butter.
2. Season the chicken with ½ teaspoon of salt and the pepper. Place the chicken in the skillet and cook over medium heat for 3 to 4 minutes. Flip the chicken and cook for an additional 3 to 4 minutes, or until fully cooked. Transfer the chicken to a plate and set aside.
3. Add the garlic to the skillet and sauté for 1 minute, or until fragrant. Pour in the chicken broth and simmer until the liquid reduces by half, about 4 minutes.
4. While the broth simmers, combine the cauliflower rice, water, and the remaining ½ teaspoon of salt in a microwave-safe bowl. Cover with plastic wrap and microwave on high for about 3 minutes, or until the cauliflower is tender. Stir and drain any excess liquid.
5. Turn off the heat under the skillet and add the remaining 2 tablespoons of cold butter. Swirl the skillet gently to melt the butter and thicken the sauce slightly.
6. Return the chicken to the skillet along with any juices from the plate, and top with the parsley and paprika.
7. Serve the chicken with a generous spoonful of sauce on a bed of cauliflower rice.
8. Refrigerate in an airtight container for up to 5 days.
Per Serving: Calories 259; Fat 12.12g; Sodium 1050mg; Carbs 5.15g; Fiber 1.8g; Sugar 1.63g; Protein 34.21g

Turkey Lettuce Wraps

Prep Time: 20 minutes | Cook Time: 10 minutes | Serves: 4

1 tablespoon avocado oil
2 tablespoons peeled and grated fresh ginger
1 garlic clove, minced
1 pound lean ground turkey
¼ cup low-sodium chicken broth
1 tablespoon sugar-free fish sauce (optional but highly suggested)
2 tablespoons lime juice
1 teaspoon brown sugar substitute
1 tablespoon natural peanut butter
8 large lettuce leaves, romaine, butter lettuce or iceberg
Garnishes: Cilantro, bean sprouts, sliced scallions, sliced jalapeños, or sliced bird's eye chile.

1. Heat the oil in a large skillet over medium heat. Add the ginger and garlic and cook for 1 to 2 minutes, until fragrant; be careful not to let them burn.
2. Add the ground turkey, and use a spatula to break it up and mix it with the ginger and garlic. Cook for 5 to 6 minutes or until the turkey is no longer pink and much of the liquid has evaporated.
3. Meanwhile, in a small bowl, combine the chicken broth, fish sauce, lime juice, and peanut butter. Add this mixture to the ground turkey and cook for 2 to 3 minutes, or until most of the liquid has evaporated.
4. Add ⅓ cup of the turkey mixture to a lettuce cup, top it with your favorite garnishes, and enjoy.
5. Refrigerate leftovers in an airtight container for up to 5 days.
Per Serving: Calories 229; Fat 13.84g; Sodium 149mg; Carbs 4.62g; Fiber 0.5g; Sugar 2.68g; Protein 22.25g

Feta & Sun-Dried Tomato Stuffed Chicken Breasts

Prep Time: 15 minutes | Cook Time: 25 minutes | Serves: 2

Nonstick cooking spray
2 (5-ounce) boneless, skinless chicken breasts
2 ounces crumbled feta cheese
2 tablespoons chopped oil-packed sun-dried tomatoes
½ teaspoon finely chopped fresh basil
¼ teaspoon minced garlic
Sea salt
Freshly ground black pepper

1. Preheat the oven to 400°F. Lightly coat a 9-inch square baking dish with cooking spray and set it aside.
2. Create a pocket in the center of each chicken breast by slicing it lengthwise.
3. In a small bowl, mix the feta, sun-dried tomatoes, basil, and garlic until well combined.
4. Spoon the filling into the chicken breasts and close the pocket by pressing the edges together and sealing the pockets with wooden toothpicks. Season the breasts with salt and pepper.
5. Place the stuffed breasts into the prepared dish and bake until the chicken is cooked through, about 25 minutes. Remove the toothpicks and serve.

Per Serving: Calories: 255; Fat: 10g; Carbs: 3g; Sodium: 332mg; Fiber: 1g; Protein: 36g

Lemon Herb Chicken Breast

Prep Time: 10 minutes | Cook Time: 25 minutes | Serves: 4

Nonstick cooking spray
4 boneless, skinless chicken breasts (about 4 oz each)
1 tablespoon olive oil
1 teaspoon garlic powder
1 teaspoon dried oregano
1 teaspoon dried thyme
Zest and juice of 1 lemon
¼ teaspoon salt
¼ teaspoon freshly ground black pepper

1. Preheat the oven to 375°F. Coat a baking dish with nonstick cooking spray.
2. In a small bowl, mix olive oil, garlic powder, oregano, thyme, lemon zest, lemon juice, salt, and pepper.
3. Evenly coat the chicken breasts with the mixture and place them in the baking dish.
4. Bake for 20-25 minutes, or until the internal temperature reaches 165°F.
5. Let rest for 5 minutes before serving.

Per Serving: Calories 180; Fat 6g; Sodium 250mg; Carbs 2g; Fiber 1g; Sugar 0g; Protein 26g

Spicy Grilled Chicken Thighs

Prep Time: 10 minutes | Cook Time: 20 minutes | Serves: 4

Nonstick cooking spray
4 boneless, skinless chicken thighs (about 4 oz each)
1 tablespoon smoked paprika
1 teaspoon chili powder
½ teaspoon garlic powder
½ teaspoon onion powder
¼ teaspoon cayenne pepper (optional)
¼ teaspoon salt
¼ teaspoon freshly ground black pepper

1. Preheat a grill or grill pan to medium-high heat. Lightly coat with nonstick cooking spray.
2. In a small bowl, mix smoked paprika, chili powder, garlic powder, onion powder, cayenne pepper, salt, and black pepper.
3. Rub the spice mixture evenly over the chicken thighs.
4. Grill the chicken for 8-10 minutes per side, or until the internal temperature reaches 165°F.
5. Let rest for 5 minutes before serving.

Per Serving: Calories 170; Fat 7g; Sodium 230mg; Carbs 2g; Fiber 1g; Sugar 0g; Protein 24g

Baked Parmesan Chicken Tenders

Prep Time: 15 minutes | Cook Time: 20 minutes | Serves: 4

Nonstick cooking spray
1 lb chicken tenders (about 8 tenders)
½ teaspoon garlic powder
½ teaspoon onion powder
¼ teaspoon salt
¼ teaspoon freshly ground black pepper
1 large egg
2 tablespoons unsweetened almond milk
¼ cup grated Parmesan cheese
4 tablespoons whole-wheat bread crumbs

1. Preheat the oven to 400°F. Coat a baking sheet with nonstick cooking spray.
2. Season the chicken tenders with garlic powder, onion powder, salt, and pepper.
3. In a shallow bowl, whisk together the egg and almond milk. In another shallow bowl, combine the Parmesan cheese and bread crumbs.
4. Dip each chicken tender into the egg mixture, then coat with the bread crumb mixture. Arrange them on the prepared baking sheet.
5. Bake for 15-20 minutes, flipping halfway through, until the coating turns golden brown and the chicken is fully cooked.

Per Serving: Calories 190; Fat 5g; Sodium 320mg; Carbs 5g; Fiber 1g; Sugar 1g; Protein 28g

Easy Beef Burgers

Prep Time: 20 minutes | Cook Time: 10 minutes | Serves: 4

1 tsp. dried parsley
1 tsp. onion powder
1 tsp. oregano, dried
½ tsp. garlic powder
1 pound lean ground beef
1 tsp. sea salt

1. Preheat the air fryer to 350°F for at least five minutes.
2. Stir together the seasonings in a medium-sized mixing bowl. Add the beef and use your hands to mix, making sure not to overwork.
3. Divide up the meat into four burger patties, placing a small indent with your thumb in the center of each patty to make sure they don't get too thick and pink in the middle.
4. Place the burger patties in the air fryer tray. Cook the burgers in the air fryer for 10 minutes to achieve "medium," or a bit longer if you want medium-well or well burgers.
5. Serve the burgers warm, and enjoy.
Per Serving: Calories 247; Fat 12.61g; Sodium 651mg; Carbs 0.96g; Fiber 0.2g; Sugar 0g; Protein 30.35g

Beef & Brown Rice Stuffed Cabbage Rolls

Prep Time: 15 minutes | Cook Time: 33 minutes | Serves: 4

1 head green cabbage
1 pound lean ground beef
½ cup long-grain brown rice
4 garlic cloves, minced
1 teaspoon salt
½ teaspoon black pepper
1 teaspoon ground cinnamon
2 tablespoons chopped fresh mint
Juice of 1 lemon
Olive oil cooking spray
½ cup beef broth
1 tablespoon olive oil

1. Slice the cabbage in half and remove the core. Remove 12 of the larger leaves to use for the cabbage rolls.
2. Bring a large pot of salted water to a boil, then drop the cabbage leaves into the water, boiling them for 3 minutes. Remove from the water and set aside.
3. In a large bowl, combine the ground beef, rice, garlic, salt, pepper, cinnamon, mint, and lemon juice, and mix together until combined. Divide this mixture into 12 equal portions.
4. Preheat the air fryer to 360°F. Lightly coat a small casserole dish with olive oil cooking spray.
5. Lay a cabbage leaf on a clean work surface. Place a spoonful of the beef mixture on one side of the leaf, leaving space on all other sides. Fold the two perpendicular sides inward and then roll forward, tucking tightly as rolled (similar to a burrito roll). Place the finished rolls into the baking dish, stacking them on top of each other if needed.
6. Pour the beef broth over the top of the cabbage rolls so that it soaks down between them, and then brush the tops with the olive oil.
7. Place the casserole dish into the air fryer basket and bake for 30 minutes.
Per Serving: Calories: 329; Total Fat: 10g; Saturated Fat: 3g; Protein: 29g; Total Carbohydrates: 33g; Fiber: 7g; Sugar: 8g; Cholesterol: 70mg

Slow-Cooked Pork Loin and Apple

Prep Time: 10 minutes | Cook Time: 6 hours | Serves: 8

1 (2-pound) pork tenderloin
½ teaspoon salt
½ teaspoon freshly ground black pepper
3 teaspoons ground cinnamon, divided
1 tablespoon organic canola oil
2 onions, cut into 6 wedges each
3 firm apples (such as Honeycrisp or Fuji), cored and cut into wedges
¼ cup water

1. Cut 8 to 10 slits about 1-inch-deep on one side of the pork tenderloin. Sprinkle the sides of the tenderloin with the salt, pepper, and 1 teaspoon of cinnamon.
2. In a large skillet, heat the oil over medium-high heat. Brown the tenderloin on all sides.
3. Place the onion wedges and a few apple wedges at the base of the slow cooker. Evenly sprinkle the remaining 2 teaspoons of cinnamon over them. Pour in the water. Place the tenderloin on top of the onions and apples and stuff the remaining apples into the slits of the pork. Cover and cook on low for 6 hours. Slice the pork and serve with the onions and apples.
Per Serving: Calories 251; Fat 6g; Sodium 277mg; Carbs 17g; Fiber 4g; Sugar 11g; Protein 33g

Pork Tenderloin with Cherry Sauce

Prep Time: 15 minutes | Cook Time: 25 minutes | Serves: 4

1 pork tenderloin (1 to 1¼ lb), cut into ½-inch slices
½ teaspoon garlic-pepper blend
2 teaspoons olive oil
¾ cup cherry preserves
2 tablespoons chopped shallots
1 tablespoon Dijon mustard
1 tablespoon balsamic vinegar
1 clove garlic, finely chopped

1. Coat both sides of the pork with garlic-pepper blend.
2. Heat 1 teaspoon of oil in a 12-inch skillet over medium-high heat. Add the pork and cook for 6 to 8 minutes, flipping once, until browned and a meat thermometer reads 145°F at the center. Remove the pork from the skillet and keep warm.
3. In the same skillet, add the remaining teaspoon of oil, along with the preserves, mustard, shallots, vinegar, and garlic. Stir to loosen any browned bits from the bottom of the skillet. Bring to a boil, then lower the heat and simmer uncovered for 10 minutes or until the sauce reduces to about ½ cup.
4. Pour the sauce over the pork slices before serving.
Per Serving: Calories 330; Total Fat 7g (Saturated Fat 2g, Trans Fat 0g); Cholesterol 50mg; Sodium 170mg; Total Carbohydrate 44g (Dietary Fiber 1g, Sugars 30g); Protein 23g

Beef and Zucchini Stew

Prep Time: 10 minutes | Cook Time: 4 to 6 hours | Serves: 8

5 medium zucchinis, sliced
2 lbs. beef stew meat, cubed
2 yellow onions, chopped
28 oz. can diced tomatoes
8 oz. tomato sauce
Salt and pepper to taste

1. Add all the ingredients to the slow cooker and cover with the lid. Cook on the low setting for 4 to 6 hours. Season with salt, pepper, or fresh herbs to taste.
2. Serve warm with cauliflower or any of your favorite sides.
Per Serving: Calories 293; Fat 8.69g; Sodium 840mg; Carbs 9.81g; Fiber 3.7g; Sugar 6.33g; Protein 43.37g

Beef Meatloaf

Prep Time: 15 minutes | Cook Time: 25 minutes | Serves: 6

1 pound lean ground beef
2 eggs
2 Roma tomatoes, diced
½ white onion, diced
½ cup whole wheat bread crumbs
1 teaspoon garlic powder
1 teaspoon dried oregano
1 teaspoon dried thyme
1 teaspoon salt
1 teaspoon black pepper
2 ounces fat-free mozzarella cheese, shredded
1 tablespoon olive oil
Fresh chopped parsley, for garnish

1. Preheat the oven to 380°F.
2. In a large bowl, mix together the ground beef, eggs, onion, tomatoes, bread crumbs, garlic powder, thyme, oregano, salt, pepper, and cheese.
3. Form into a loaf, flattening to 1-inch thick.
4. Brush the top with olive oil, then place the meatloaf into the air fryer basket and cook for 25 minutes.
5. Take it out of the air fryer and let it rest for 5 minutes. Then, slice and serve, garnished with a sprinkle of parsley.

Per Serving: Calories: 220; Total Fat: 10g; Saturated Fat: 4g; Protein: 22g; Total Carbohydrates: 10g; Fiber: 1g; Sugar: 2g; Cholesterol: 116mg

Spicy Beef Spinach Stuffed Peppers

Prep Time: 20 minutes | Cook Time: 22 minutes | Serves: 2

5 green or red peppers
½ pound lean ground beef
½ tsp. cayenne pepper
½ tsp. ground pepper
1 cup spinach
½ tsp. chili powder
1 tbsp. pine nuts, crushed up
1 tsp. paprika

1. Preheat the air fryer to 415°F.
2. Place the ground beef in a skillet over the stove. Cook until the beef is no longer pink, stirring occasionally.
3. While the beef cooks, slice the peppers in half and take out the insides. For one of the peppers, chop it into fine, bite-sized pieces
4. When the beef is nearly finished, add the spinach to the skillet and allow it to wilt. Add the green pepper as well, along with the spices—the chili powder, cayenne, ground pepper, and the cumin.
5. After cooking this mixture for five minutes, stuff the green or red peppers with the ground beef mixture. Top each of the peppers with pine nuts.
6. Place the stuffed peppers in the air fryer and cook them for 17 minutes, or until the vegetables are very nearly soft.
7. Serve the stuffed peppers warm, and enjoy.

Per Serving: Calories 303; Fat 13.29g; Sodium 111mg; Carbs 13.49g; Fiber 3g; Sugar 6.59g; Protein 33.42g

Pork Tenderloin and Asparagus Stir-Fry

Prep Time: 15 minutes | Cook Time: 10 minutes | Serves: 4

2 tbsp. olive oil, add more only if needed
1 pound pork tenderloin, membranes removed, sliced into ⅛-inch thick matchsticks
½ pound thick-stemmed asparagus, tough ends removed, sliced into 1½-inch long slivers
1 large white onion, peeled, thinly sliced
½ piece small red bell pepper, deseeded, ribbed, sliced into ⅛-inch thick matchsticks
½ piece small orange/yellow/green bell pepper, deseeded, ribbed, sliced into ⅛-inch thick matchsticks
sea salt and black pepper, to taste
For Garnish (all optional):
1 small lime, sliced into 6 to 8 wedges, pips removed
¼ cup fresh cilantro, minced

1. Lightly season the pork tenderloin with salt and black pepper; set aside.
2. Pour oil into non-stick wok set over medium heat. When the oil is hot enough, add in and stir-fry pork tenderloin. Cook until meat is seared brown on all sides.
3. Except for asparagus, add in remaining ingredients. Stir-fry until onions turn limp and transparent. Add in asparagus slivers. Stir. Immediately remove wok from heat.
4. Secure lid; let dish rest for 2 minutes before serving. Taste; adjust seasoning, if needed.
5. Ladle equal portions of the dish into plates. Garnish with equal portions of cilantro and lime wedge, if using. Squeeze lime juice on top of the dish before eating.
Per Serving: Calories 253; Fat 10.86g; Sodium 214mg; Carbs 6.77g; Fiber 2g; Sugar 3.23g; Protein 31.56g

Beef and Vegetable Stew

Prep Time: 15 minutes | Cook Time: 8 hours | Serves: 8

6 pieces large leeks, roots trimmed, sliced into inch-long slivers
1 piece large tomato, deseeded, quartered
1 piece small onion, peeled, quartered
1 piece small red bell pepper, ribbed, deseeded, cubed
3 cups water
2 cups loosely packed napa cabbage, sliced into inch-thick slivers
2 pounds beef, hanger steak, sliced into inch-thick cubes
½ pound green beans, ends, and strings removed, sliced into inch-long slivers
1 can (15 oz.) straw mushrooms, rinsed, drained well
1 can (8 oz.) water chestnuts, rinsed, drained well
Sea salt, to taste
Optional:
1 tbsp. green or red peppercorns

1. Except for green beans and napa cabbage, place remaining ingredients into slow cooker on low heat. Secure lid. Cook for 8 hours.
2. Add remaining ingredients. Turn off heat. Stir. Taste; adjust seasoning, if needed.
3. Rest the stew for 5 minutes prior to serving. Ladle into individual bowls. Serve.
Per Serving: Calories 261; Fat 7.51g; Sodium 412mg; Carbs 23.5g; Fiber 4.2g; Sugar 5.13g; Protein 27.38g

Beef and Rutabaga Stew

Prep Time: 20 minutes | Cook Time: 1½ hours | Serves: 6

1 pound eye of round or bottom round roast, cubed
1 large onion, chopped
4 celery stalks, chopped
4 cups water or low-sodium beef or chicken broth
1 (14.5-ounce) can low-sodium diced tomatoes, drained
2 bay leaves
1 teaspoon dried oregano
1 teaspoon dried thyme
1 teaspoon salt
½ teaspoon black pepper
2 cups diced peeled rutabaga
1 cup diced peeled turnip
1 medium carrot, peeled and diced

1. Heat a large Dutch oven over medium-high heat. Add the beef and sear all sides until they are nicely browned.
2. Add the onion and celery to the pot, sautéing until they start to soften. Then, add the water, tomatoes, bay leaves, oregano, thyme, salt, and pepper. Bring the mixture to a boil, then lower the heat, cover, and let it simmer for 45 minutes.
3. Add the rutabaga, turnip, and carrot. Cook until the vegetables are tender and the beef breaks apart easily, about 40 minutes.
4. Turn off the heat and let the stew sit for 10 minutes. Using a large spoon, skim the layer of fat from the top of the stew and discard. Serve hot.
Per Serving: Calories 203; Fat 5g; Sodium 563mg; Carbs 15g; Fiber 4g; Sugar 8g; Protein 24g

Garlic Beef and Cauliflower

Prep Time: 15 minutes | Cook Time: 15 minutes | Serves: 4

1 tablespoon avocado oil
1 pound 93% lean ground beef
¼ cup sliced yellow onion
1 tablespoon peeled and minced fresh ginger
1 garlic clove, minced
¼ cup low-sodium beef broth
4 cups cauliflower florets (about 2 large crowns)
2 tablespoons coconut aminos (or soy sauce)
¼ teaspoon kosher salt
½ teaspoon sesame seeds, for garnishing

1. Heat the oil in a large skillet or wok over medium heat. Add the ground beef and cook, using a wooden spoon or spatula to break it into smaller pieces, for about 4 minutes, or until it is partially cooked.
2. Add the onion, ginger, and garlic, and cook for 2 to 3 minutes or until the beef is no longer pink. Spoon out any excess fat from the skillet and discard it.
3. Add the beef broth and cauliflower to the ground beef, increase the heat to medium-high, and cook for 2 to 3 minutes or until the cauliflower is tender.
4. Stir in the coconut aminos and salt. Adjust the seasonings if necessary, then top with the sesame seeds and serve.
5. Refrigerate the leftovers in an airtight container for 3 to 4 days.
Per Serving: Calories 326; Fat 17.82g; Sodium 370mg; Carbs 8.27g; Fiber 2.4g; Sugar 3.32g; Protein 32.62g

Basil Goulash with Eggplant

Prep Time: 20 minutes | Cook Time: 15 minutes | Serves: 6

2 tablespoons olive oil, divided
6 cloves garlic, chopped
2 medium eggplant, cut into 1-inch cubes
¾ cup fresh basil, chopped + extra to garnish
3 tablespoons tomato paste
3 shallots, chopped
1½ pounds lean ground beef
1½ cans (14 ounces each) diced tomatoes
3 teaspoons salt or to taste
¼ cup coconut cream

1. Heat a large saucepan over medium heat. Add half the oil. When the oil is heated, add shallots and garlic and sauté until translucent.
2. Add beef and cook until brown. Drain excess fat in the pan and add tomatoes with its juice, salt, and basil. Lower heat.
3. Meanwhile, place another saucepan over medium heat. Add remaining oil. When the oil is heated, add eggplants and cook until tender. Transfer into the beef mixture.
4. Add coconut cream and tomato paste and stir well.
5. Sprinkle some basil on top and serve.
Per Serving: Calories 384; Fat 21.08g; Sodium 1297mg; Carbs 16.48g; Fiber 7.2g; Sugar 9.07g; Protein 33.47g

Savory Shredded Beef

Prep Time: 10 minutes | Cook Time: 9 hours | Serves: 6

¼ tsp. chili powder
½ tsp. white pepper

½ tsp. black pepper
½ tsp. paprika
1 tsp. garlic powder
1 tsp. salt
1 onion, yellow
½ cup chicken broth
2 lbs. strip steak

1. Slice up the yellow onions. Bring out the slow cooker and get it set up so that it is cooking at a low heat.
2. Take the strip steak and place it into the slow cooker along with the chicken broth and the onions to start.
3. When those are nicely arranged, add the white pepper, chili powder, paprika, black pepper, salt, and garlic powder.
4. Cover the slow cooker with lid and let these ingredients cook for 9 hours on a low setting.
5. When this time is up, take out two forks and use them to shred up the steak. Serve with some vegetable and enjoy.
Per Serving: Calories 245; Fat 5.97g; Sodium 1059mg; Carbs 2.64g; Fiber 0.6g; Sugar 0.91g; Protein 45.27g

Meatballs with Zoodles

Prep Time: 20 minutes | Cook Time: 25 minutes | Serves: 4

For the Meatballs:
8 ounces lean ground beef
½ cup cooked quinoa
2 tablespoons finely chopped onion
¼ cup grated carrot
1 garlic clove, minced
½ teaspoon freshly ground black pepper
1 large egg, lightly beaten
For the Marinara:
2 tablespoons extra-virgin olive oil
2 garlic cloves, minced
1 (28-ounce) can crushed tomatoes
1 teaspoon honey
½ teaspoon salt
Pinch freshly ground black pepper
For the Zoodles:
4 medium zucchini
2 tablespoons extra-virgin olive oil, divided

To make the meatballs:

1. Preheat the oven to 450°F. Line a baking sheet with parchment paper and set aside.

2. In a large bowl, combine all the meatballs ingredients and mix well. Using your hands, shape the meat into 12 small, firmly packed balls, and transfer them to the lined baking sheet.

3. Bake for approximately 15 minutes, or until fully cooked and golden brown.

To make the marinara:

1. While the meatballs are baking, heat the olive oil in a small pot over medium heat. Add the garlic and sauté for 1 minute, or until it starts to turn golden brown.

2. Stir in the tomatoes, honey, salt, and pepper, then let the mixture simmer for about 10 minutes to allow the flavors to blend.

To make the zoodles:

1. Use a spiralizer to cut the zucchini into noodles, each about 4 to 6 inches long.

2. Heat 1 tablespoon of olive oil in a pan over medium-high heat. Add half of the zoodles. Using tongs, stir the zoodles around the pan. Continue to stir until the zoodles become slightly tender, about 2 minutes' total. Transfer to a bowl. Repeat with the remaining zoodles and oil.

3. Divide the zoodles among four plates and top each with 3 meatballs and some marinara.

Per Serving: Calories 272; Fat 14.55g; Sodium 712mg; Carbs 16.36g; Fiber 5.2g; Sugar 7.62g; Protein 20g

Roasted Salmon with Lemon Zest & Parsley

Prep Time: 10 minutes | Cook Time: 10 minutes | Serves: 6

1½ pounds skin-on salmon fillet, cut into 4 pieces
1 teaspoon sea salt, divided
¼ teaspoon freshly ground black pepper
3 tablespoons extra-virgin olive oil
1 bunch fresh Italian parsley leaves, finely chopped
1 garlic clove, minced
Zest of 1 lemon, finely grated

1. Preheat the oven to 350°F.
2. Season the salmon with ½ teaspoon of salt and the pepper.
3. In a large, ovenproof skillet over medium-high heat, heat the olive oil until it shimmers.
4. Place the salmon in the skillet, skin-side down. Cook for about 5 minutes, gently pressing on the salmon with a spatula, until the skin crisps. Transfer the pan to the oven and cook the salmon for 3 to 4 minutes more until it is opaque.
5. In a small bowl, stir together the parsley, garlic, lemon zest, and remaining ½ teaspoon of sea salt. Sprinkle the mixture over the salmon and serve.

Per Serving: Calories: 214; Protein: 22g; Total Carbohydrates: <1g; Sugars: <1g; Fiber: <1g; Total Fat: 14g; Saturated Fat: 2g; Cholesterol: 50mg; Sodium: 522mg

Baked Fish with Tomato and Olive

Prep Time: 10 minutes | Cook Time: 25 minutes | Serves: 4

2 tablespoons olive oil
½ onion, chopped
2 shallots, diced
4 garlic cloves, minced
1 (28-ounce) can diced tomatoes, drained
Sea salt
Freshly ground black pepper
1 pound cod or other white-fleshed fish
½ cup chopped pitted kalamata olives
¼ cup crumbled feta cheese, for topping
¼ cup chopped fresh Italian parsley (optional)

1. Preheat the oven to 375°F.
2. In a large oven-safe skillet, heat the olive oil over medium-high heat. Add the onion, shallots, and garlic and sauté for 5 to 6 minutes, until softened. Add the tomatoes and season with salt and pepper. Cook, stirring occasionally, for 4 minutes.
3. Place the fish on top of the tomato mixture and evenly sprinkle with the olives and feta. Transfer the skillet to the oven and bake for 15 to 20 minutes, until the fish is cooked through.
4. Garnish with the parsley, if desired, and serve.

Per Serving: Calories: 229; Total fat: 12g; Total carbs: 12g; Sugar: 6g; Protein: 21g; Fiber: 5g; Sodium: 724mg

Lemon Roasted Sea Bass with Root Vegetables

Prep Time: 15 minutes | Cook Time: 15 minutes | Serves: 4

1 carrot, diced small
1 parsnip, diced small
1 rutabaga, diced small
¼ cup olive oil
2 teaspoons salt, divided
4 sea bass fillets
½ teaspoon onion powder
2 garlic cloves, minced
1 lemon, sliced, plus additional wedges for serving

1. Preheat the air fryer to 380°F.
2. In a small bowl, toss the carrot, parsnip, and rutabaga with olive oil and 1 teaspoon salt.
3. Lightly season the sea bass with the remaining 1 teaspoon of salt and the onion powder, then place it into the air fryer basket in a single layer.
4. Spread the garlic over the top of each fillet, then cover with lemon slices.
5. Pour the prepared vegetables into the basket around and on top of the fish. Roast for 15 minutes.
6. Serve with additional lemon wedges if desired.
Per Serving: Calories: 299; Total Fat: 16g; Saturated Fat: 3g; Protein: 25g; Total Carbohydrates: 13g; Fiber: 3g; Sugar: 5g; Cholesterol: 53mg

Smoked Salmon on Cucumber Disks

Prep Time: 15 minutes | Serves: 4

1 piece large cucumber, ends removed, sliced diagonally into ⅛-inch thick disks/medallions
For Salad:
10 oz. smoked salmon, thinly sliced, preferably the same width of cucumber disks or slightly smaller[13]
2 tbsp. extra virgin olive oil
1 tsp. fresh dill fronds, minced
1 small lime, freshly sliced, pips removed
½ cup arugula leaves, rinsed, spun-dried, julienned
⅛ cup fresh chives, minced, reserve some for garnish
Sea salt and white pepper, to taste

1. Place cucumber slices on a serving tray lined with parchment paper. Chill disks well prior to use.
2. Except for smoked salmon and garnish, place salad ingredients into large bowl. Mix well. Taste; adjust seasoning, if needed.
3. Spoon equal portions salad on top of cucumber disks; layer smoked salmon slices on top.
4. Garnish with remaining chives. Serve immediately.
Per Serving: Calories 157; Fat 8.29g; Sodium 370mg; Carbs 5.17g; Fiber 0.8g; Sugar 2g; Protein 15.58g

Grilled Lemon Mahi Mahi

Prep Time: 30 minutes | Cook Time: 10 minutes | Serves: 2

¾ pound mahi-mahi
1 tablespoon ghee or olive oil
½ teaspoon dried thyme
Salt to taste
1½ tablespoons lemon juice
1 clove garlic, minced
¼ teaspoon pepper or to taste

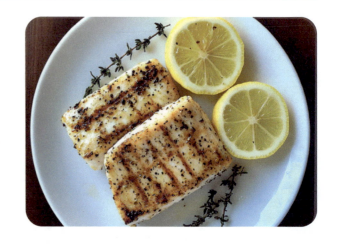

1. Place fish in a dish. Mix together rest of the ingredients into a bowl and pour over the fish. Set aside for 30 minutes.
2. Grill on a preheated grill for 4-5 minutes on each side or flaky when pierced with a fork. You can also broil in an oven.
Per Serving: Calories 184; Fat 7.5g; Sodium 865mg; Carbs 1.87g; Fiber 0.2g; Sugar 0.59g; Protein 26.23g

Lemon-Garlic Trout

Prep Time: 10 minutes | Cook Time: 15 minutes | Serves: 4

4 trout fillets
2 tablespoons olive oil
2 garlic cloves, sliced
½ teaspoon salt
1 teaspoon black pepper
1 lemon, sliced, plus more wedges for serving

1. Preheat the air fryer to 380°F.
2. Brush each fillet with olive oil on both sides and season with salt and pepper. Place the fillets in an even layer in the air fryer basket.
3. Arrange the sliced garlic on top of the trout fillets, then place lemon slices over the garlic. Cook for 12 to 15 minutes, or until the internal temperature reaches 145°F.
4. Serve with fresh lemon wedges.
Per Serving: Calories: 231; Total Fat: 12g; Saturated Fat: 2g; Protein: 29g; Total Carbohydrates: 1g; Fiber: 0g; Sugar: 0g; Cholesterol: 84mg

Lemon Herb Baked Cod

Prep Time: 10 minutes | Cook Time: 20 minutes | Serves: 4

Nonstick cooking spray
4 cod fillets (about 4 oz each)
1 tablespoon olive oil
1 teaspoon garlic powder
1 teaspoon dried oregano
1 teaspoon dried thyme
Zest and juice of 1 lemon
¼ teaspoon salt
¼ teaspoon freshly ground black pepper

1. Preheat the oven to 375°F. Coat a baking dish with nonstick cooking spray.
2. In a small bowl, mix olive oil, garlic powder, oregano, thyme, lemon zest, lemon juice, salt, and pepper.
3. Rub the mixture evenly over the cod fillets and place them in the baking dish.
4. Bake for 15-20 minutes, or until the fish flakes easily with a fork.
5. Let rest for 5 minutes before serving.
Per Serving: Calories 150; Fat 5g; Sodium 220mg; Carbs 2g; Fiber 1g; Sugar 0g; Protein 23g

Dill Roasted Whole Red Snapper

Prep Time: 10 minutes | Cook Time: 35 minutes | Serves: 4

1 teaspoon salt
½ teaspoon black pepper
½ teaspoon ground cumin
¼ teaspoon cayenne
1 (1 to 1½-pound) whole red snapper, cleaned and patted dry
2 tablespoons olive oil
2 garlic cloves, minced
¼ cup fresh dill
Lemon wedges, for serving

1. Preheat the air fryer to 360°F.
2. In a small bowl, mix together the salt, pepper, cumin, and cayenne.
3. Coat the outside of the fish with olive oil, then sprinkle the seasoning blend over the outside of the fish. Stuff the minced garlic and dill inside the cavity of the fish.
4. Arrange the snapper in the air fryer basket and roast for 20 minutes. Flip the snapper over, and roast for 15 minutes more, or until the snapper reaches an internal temperature of 145°F. Serve with lemon wedges.
Per Serving: Calories: 125; Total Fat: 2g; Saturated Fat: 0g; Protein: 23g; Total Carbohydrates: 2g; Fiber: 0g; Sugar: 0g; Cholesterol: 42mg

Tuna and Zucchini Burgers

Prep Time: 20 minutes | Cook Time: 12 minutes | Serves: 4

3 slices whole-wheat sandwich bread, toasted
2 (5-ounce) cans tuna in olive oil, drained
1 cup shredded zucchini (about ¾ small zucchini)
1 large egg, lightly beaten
¼ cup diced red bell pepper (about ¼ pepper)
1 tablespoon dried oregano
1 teaspoon lemon zest
¼ teaspoon freshly ground black pepper
¼ teaspoon kosher or sea salt
1 tablespoon extra-virgin olive oil
Salad greens or 4 whole-wheat rolls, for serving (optional)

1. Crumble the toast into bread crumbs using your fingers (or use a knife to cut into ¼-inch cubes) until you have 1 cup of loosely packed crumbs. Pour the crumbs into a large bowl. Add the tuna, egg, zucchini, bell pepper, lemon zest, oregano, black pepper, and salt. Mix well with a fork. With your hands, form the mixture into four (½-cup-size) patties. Place on a plate, and press each patty flat to about ¾-inch thick.
2. In a large skillet over medium-high heat, heat the oil until it's very hot, about 2 minutes. Add the patties to the hot oil, then turn the heat down to medium. Cook the patties for 5 minutes, flip with a spatula, and cook for an additional 5 minutes. Enjoy as is or serve on salad greens or whole-wheat rolls.

Per Serving: Calories: 191; Total Fat: 10g; Saturated Fat: 2g; Cholesterol: 72mg; Sodium: 472mg; Total Carbohydrates: 11g; Fiber: 2g; Protein: 15g

Orange Shrimp Salad

Prep Time: 15 minutes | Cook Time: 10 minutes | Serves: 6

1 large orange
3 tablespoons extra-virgin olive oil, divided
1 tablespoon chopped fresh rosemary (about 3 sprigs) or 1 teaspoon dried rosemary
1 tablespoon chopped fresh thyme (about 6 sprigs) or 1 teaspoon dried thyme
3 garlic cloves, minced (about 1½ teaspoons)
¼ teaspoon freshly ground black pepper
¼ teaspoon kosher or sea salt
1½ pounds fresh raw shrimp, (or frozen and thawed raw shrimp) shells and tails removed

1. Zest the entire orange using a microplane or citrus grater.
2. In a large zip-top plastic bag, combine the orange zest and 2 tablespoons of oil with the rosemary, thyme, garlic, pepper, and salt. Add the shrimp to a resealable bag, seal it, and gently massage the bag to ensure the shrimp are coated evenly with the seasonings. Set it aside.
3. Heat a large skillet over medium heat. Heat the remaining 1 tablespoon of oil in the skillet. Add half of the shrimp and cook for 4 to 6 minutes, stirring every minute, until they turn pink and white. Transfer the shrimp to a large serving bowl. Repeat with the remaining shrimp and add them to the bowl.
4. While the shrimp cook, cut the orange flesh into bite-size pieces. Add to the serving bowl, and toss with the cooked shrimp. Serve immediately or refrigerate and serve cold.

Per Serving: Calories: 190; Total Fat: 8g; Saturated Fat: 1g; Cholesterol: 221mg; Sodium: 215mg; Total Carbohydrates: 4g; Fiber: 1g; Protein: 24g

Shrimp Puttanesca

Prep Time: 5 minutes | Cook Time: 15 minutes | Serves: 4

2 tablespoons extra-virgin olive oil
3 anchovy fillets, drained and chopped (half a 2-ounce tin), or 1½ teaspoons anchovy paste
3 garlic cloves, minced
½ teaspoon crushed red pepper
1 (14.5-ounce) can low-sodium or no-salt-added diced tomatoes, undrained
1 (2.25-ounce) can sliced black olives, drained (about ½ cup)
2 tablespoons capers
1 teaspoon dried oregano or 1 tablespoon chopped fresh oregano
1 pound fresh raw shrimp (or frozen and thawed shrimp), shells and tails removed

1. In a large skillet over medium heat, heat the oil. Mix in the anchovies, garlic, and crushed red pepper. Cook for 3 minutes, stirring frequently and mashing up the anchovies with a wooden spoon, until they have melted into the oil.
2. Stir in the tomatoes with their juices, olives, capers, and oregano. Turn up the heat to medium-high, and bring to a simmer.
3. When the sauce is lightly bubbling, stir in the shrimp. Reduce the heat to medium, and cook the shrimp for 6 to 8 minutes, or until they turn pink and white, stirring occasionally, and serve.
Per Serving: Calories: 214; Total Fat: 10g; Saturated Fat: 2g; Cholesterol: 178mg; Sodium: 553mg; Total Carbohydrates: 7g; Fiber: 2g; Protein: 26g

Cajun Salmon Po'boy

Prep Time: 20 minutes | Cook Time: 10 minutes | Serves: 4

4 (4-ounce) skinless salmon fillets
2 teaspoons Cajun seasoning
2 teaspoons olive oil
1 cup finely shredded cabbage
1 large carrot, shredded
1 scallion, both white and green parts, sliced
¼ cup low-fat plain Greek yogurt
1 tablespoon apple cider vinegar
1 teaspoon maple syrup
4 crusty whole-wheat rolls, halved

1. Preheat the oven to 400°F.
2. Season the salmon fillets with the Cajun seasoning.
3. In a large ovenproof skillet, heat the oil over medium-high heat. Pan-sear the salmon for 2 minutes per side, then place the skillet in the oven. Roast for 6 minutes, until just cooked through. Remove the salmon from the oven and set it aside.
4. While the salmon is cooking, in a large bowl, toss the cabbage, carrot, scallion, yogurt, vinegar, and maple syrup until well combined.
5. Place a salmon fillet on each roll and top with of the cabbage mixture. Serve.
Per Serving: Calories: 326; Total fat: 11g; Saturated fat: 3g; Sodium: 276mg; Carbohydrates: 25g; Sugar: 5g; Fiber: 3g; Protein: 30g

Shrimp, Zucchini and Asparagus Stir-Fry

¼ cup freshly squeezed lemon juice
¼ cup olive oil
½ teaspoon onion powder
½ teaspoon garlic powder
14 ounces medium shrimp (36/40 count), peeled and deveined
½ onion, chopped
2 zucchinis, quartered lengthwise and sliced into ½-inch pieces
½ bunch asparagus, woody ends trimmed, chopped
1 tomato, chopped
1 garlic clove, minced
1½ teaspoons dried basil
½ teaspoon dried oregano
¼ teaspoon sea salt
¼ teaspoon freshly ground black pepper
Dash red pepper flakes
½ cup kalamata olives, pitted
¼ cup crumbled feta cheese, for topping

1. In a small bowl, stir together the lemon juice, olive oil, onion powder, and garlic powder. Add the shrimp, mix well, and cover with plastic wrap. Marinate in the refrigerator for 10 minutes.
2. Heat a large skillet over medium-high heat. Add the marinated shrimp (discard the marinade) and cook until pink, 3 to 5 minutes. Use a slotted spoon to remove the shrimp and transfer them to a medium bowl.
3. In the same skillet, sauté the onion over medium-high heat for 3 minutes. Add the asparagus, zucchini, tomato, garlic, oregano, basil, salt, black pepper, and red pepper flakes and cook for 2 to 3 minutes.
4. Return the shrimp to the skillet, add the olives, and stir to combine everything evenly.
5. Serve topped with the feta.
Per Serving: Calories: 276; Total fat: 19g; Total carbs: 11g; Sugar: 5g; Protein: 18g; Fiber: 3g; Sodium: 721mg

Lemony Salmon with Tomatoes and Olives

2 tablespoons olive oil
4 (1½-inch-thick) salmon fillets
½ teaspoon salt
¼ teaspoon cayenne
1 teaspoon chopped fresh dill
2 Roma tomatoes, halved
¼ cup sliced Kalamata olives
4 lemon slices

1. Preheat the air fryer to 380°F.
2. Brush the olive oil on both sides of the salmon fillets, and then season them lightly with salt, cayenne, and dill.
3. Place the fillets in a single layer in the basket of the air fryer, then layer the tomatoes and olives over the top. Top each fillet with a lemon slice.
4. Bake for 8 minutes, or until the internal temperature of the salmon reaches 145°F.
Per Serving: Calories: 241; Total Fat: 15g; Saturated Fat: 2g; Protein: 23g; Total Carbohydrates: 3g; Fiber: 1g; Sugar: 2g; Cholesterol: 62mg

Pan-Seared Scallops with Orange Spinach

Prep Time: 10 minutes | Cook Time: 15 minutes | Serves: 4

1 pound sea scallops
1 teaspoon sea salt, divided
½ teaspoon freshly ground black pepper, divided
2 tablespoons extra-virgin olive oil
6 cups fresh baby spinach
Juice of 1 orange
Pinch red pepper flakes

1. Season the scallops on both sides with ½ teaspoon of sea salt and ¼ teaspoon black pepper.
2. In a large skillet over medium-high heat, heat the olive oil until it shimmers.
3. Add the scallops. Cook for 3 to 4 minutes per side without moving until browned. Take the scallops out of the skillet and set them aside, loosely covering them with aluminum foil to retain their warmth.
4. Return the skillet to the heat and add the spinach, orange juice, red pepper flakes, remaining ½ teaspoon of salt, and remaining ¼ teaspoon of black pepper. Cook for 4 to 5 minutes, stirring, until the spinach wilts.
5. Divide the spinach among 4 plates and top with the scallops. Serve immediately.

Per Serving: Calories: 186; Protein: 21g; Total Carbohydrates: 8g; Sugars: 3g; Fiber: 2g; Total Fat: 8g; Saturated Fat: <1g; Cholesterol: 37mg; Sodium: 686mg

Kale and Tuna Bowl

Prep Time: 20 minutes | Cook Time: 15 minutes | Serves: 6

1 pound kale, chopped, center ribs removed (about 12 cups)
3 tablespoons extra-virgin olive oil
1 cup chopped onion (about ½ medium onion)
3 garlic cloves, minced (about 1½ teaspoons)
1 (2.25-ounce) can sliced olives, drained (about ½ cup)
¼ cup capers
¼ teaspoon crushed red pepper
2 teaspoons sugar
2 (6-ounce) cans tuna in olive oil, undrained
1 (15-ounce) can cannellini beans or great northern beans, drained and rinsed
¼ teaspoon freshly ground black pepper
¼ teaspoon kosher or sea salt

1. Fill a large stockpot three-quarters full of water, and bring to a boil. Add the kale and cook for 2 minutes. (This is to make the kale less bitter.) Transfer the kale to a colander to drain, then set it aside.
2. Place the empty pot back on the stove over medium heat and add the oil. Add the onion and cook for 4 minutes, stirring often. Add the garlic and cook for 1 minute, stirring often. Add the olives, capers, and crushed red pepper, and cook for 1 minute, stirring often. Add the partially cooked kale and sugar, stirring until the kale is completely coated with oil. Cover the pot and cook for 8 minutes.
3. Remove the kale from the heat, mix in the tuna, beans, pepper, and salt, and serve.

Per Serving: Calories: 265; Total Fat: 12g; Saturated Fat: 2g; Cholesterol: 21mg; Sodium: 710mg; Total Carbohydrates: 26g; Fiber: 7g; Protein: 16g

Spicy Halibut with Olives and Tomatoes

Prep Time: 20 minutes | Cook Time: 8 minutes | Serves: 4

4 (6-ounce) halibut fillets
2 tablespoons extra-virgin olive oil
½ teaspoon sea salt
¼ teaspoon freshly ground black pepper
⅛ teaspoon crushed red pepper flakes
2 garlic cloves, thinly sliced
1 cup grape tomatoes, halved
¼ cup chopped onion
2 tablespoons capers, drained
8 Kalamata olives, pitted and quartered
2 tablespoons plus 2 teaspoons dry white wine
8 fresh thyme sprigs

1. Cut 4 (15-inch) squares of parchment paper or aluminum foil. Set aside.
2. Preheat the oven to 450°F.
3. Brush the halibut with the olive oil and sprinkle with the sea salt, black pepper, and red pepper flakes. Place each fillet on a parchment square.
4. Layer the fillets with the garlic, tomatoes, onion, capers, and olives. Fold into packets, leaving the tops open.
5. Add 2 teaspoons white wine to each packet along with a thyme sprig. Seal the packets and place them on a rimmed baking sheet. Bake for about 8 minutes until the fish is opaque. Serve immediately.
Per Serving: Calories: 181; Protein: 26g; Total Carbohydrates: 3g; Sugars: 1g; Fiber: <1; Total Fat: 6g; Saturated Fat: 1g; Cholesterol: 62mg; Sodium: 383mg

Lemon Shrimp Skewers

Prep Time: 20 minutes | Cook Time: 8 minutes | Serves: 4

¼ cup olive oil
Zest and juice of 1 lemon
1 tablespoon dried oregano
¼ teaspoon red pepper flakes (optional)
Sea salt
Freshly ground black pepper
1 pound medium shrimp (36/40 count), peeled and deveined

1. In a large bowl, stir together the olive oil, lemon zest, oregano, and red pepper flakes, if desired. Season with salt and black pepper. Add the shrimp and mix well. Cover the bowl with plastic wrap and refrigerate for 15 minutes.
2. Remove the bowl from the refrigerator and thread the shrimp onto skewers. Discard any remaining marinade.
3. Heat a large skillet over medium heat. Place the skewers in the skillet and sear the shrimp for 3 to 4 minutes per side, until just cooked through.
4. Drizzle with the lemon juice and serve.
Per Serving: Calories: 204; Total fat: 15g; Total carbs: 2g; Sugar: 0g; Protein: 15g; Fiber: 0g; Sodium: 581mg

Baked Parmesan Crusted Tilapia

Prep Time: 15 minutes | Cook Time: 20 minutes | Serves: 4

Nonstick cooking spray
4 tilapia fillets (about 4 oz each)
½ teaspoon garlic powder
½ teaspoon onion powder
¼ teaspoon salt
¼ teaspoon freshly ground black pepper
1 large egg
2 tablespoons unsweetened almond milk
¼ cup grated Parmesan cheese
4 tablespoons whole-wheat bread crumbs

1. Preheat the oven to 400°F. Coat a baking sheet with nonstick cooking spray.
2. Season the tilapia fillets with garlic powder, onion powder, salt, and pepper.
3. In a shallow bowl, whisk together the egg and almond milk. In another shallow bowl, combine the Parmesan cheese and bread crumbs.
4. Coat each tilapia fillet by dipping it into the egg mixture, then rolling it in the bread crumb mixture. Place the coated fillets on the prepared baking sheet.
5. Bake for 15-20 minutes, or until the coating turns golden brown and the fish flakes easily when tested with a fork.

Per Serving: Calories 180; Fat 5g; Sodium 300mg; Carbs 5g; Fiber 1g; Sugar 1g; Protein 28g

Roasted Red Pepper and Red Lentil Dip

Prep Time: 10 minutes | Makes: 2 cups

1 (16-ounce) can red lentils, drained and rinsed
4 ounces roasted red peppers, from a jar
Juice of 1 lemon
2 tablespoons extra-virgin olive oil
1 tablespoon tahini
1 garlic clove
Sea salt

1. In a food processor, blend the lentils, roasted red peppers, lemon juice, olive oil, tahini, and garlic until smooth, stopping to scrape down the sides of the bowl as necessary.
2. Season with salt to taste.
Per Serving (⅓ cup): Calories: 129; Total fat: 6g; Saturated fat: 1g; Sodium: 86mg; Carbohydrates: 14g; Fiber: 4g; Sugar: 1g; Protein: 6g

Garlic Herb Roasted Tomatoes and Olives

Prep Time: 10 minutes | Cook Time: 20 minutes | Serves: 6

2 cups cherry tomatoes
4 garlic cloves, roughly chopped
½ red onion, roughly chopped
1 cup black olives
1 cup green olives
1 tablespoon fresh basil, minced
1 tablespoon fresh oregano, minced
2 tablespoons olive oil
¼ to ½ teaspoon salt

1. Preheat the air fryer to 380°F.
2. In a large bowl, combine all of the ingredients and toss together so that the tomatoes and olives are coated well with the olive oil and herbs.
3. Pour the mixture into the air fryer basket, and roast for 10 minutes. Stir the mixture well, then continue roasting for an additional 10 minutes.
4. Remove from the air fryer, transfer to a serving bowl, and enjoy.
Per Serving: Calories: 109; Total Fat: 10g; Saturated Fat: 1g; Protein: 1g; Total Carbohydrates: 6g; Fiber: 2g; Sugar: 2g; Cholesterol: 0mg

Kiwi Chips

Prep Time: 5 minutes | Cook Time: 12 hours | Serves: 6

6 – 8 kiwis

1. Peel all of the kiwis with a vegetable peeler and slice them into thin slices; set aside.
2. It's time to use the dehydrator. Set it to 135°F and arrange the kiwi slices inside. Let them dehydrate for approximately 12 hours until they reach a slightly chewy texture.
3. Alternatively, if using the oven, arrange the slices on a baking sheet and bake at the lowest temperature setting. Check them after four hours to monitor their progress.
Per Serving: Calories 71; Fat 0.6g; Sodium 2.3mg; Carbs 17.5g; Fiber 2.5g; Sugar 10.5g; Protein 1.2g

Zucchini Feta Roll-Ups

Prep Time: 10 minutes | Cook Time: 10 minutes | Serves: 6

½ cup feta
1 garlic clove, minced
2 tablespoons fresh basil, minced
1 tablespoon capers, minced
⅛ teaspoon salt
⅛ teaspoon red pepper flakes
1 tablespoon lemon juice
2 medium zucchini
12 toothpicks

1. Preheat the air fryer to 360°F.
2. In a small bowl, combine the feta, garlic, basil, capers, salt, red pepper flakes, and lemon juice.
3. Slice the zucchini into ⅛-inch strips lengthwise. (Each zucchini should yield around 6 strips.)
4. Spread 1 tablespoon of the cheese filling onto each slice of zucchini, then roll it up and secure it with a toothpick through the middle.
5. Place the zucchini roulades into the air fryer basket in a single layer, making sure that they don't touch each other.
6. Bake or grill in the air fryer for 10 minutes.
7. Remove the zucchini roulades from the air fryer and gently remove the toothpicks before serving.

Per Serving: Calories: 46; Total Fat: 3g; Saturated Fat: 1g; Protein: 3g; Total Carbohydrates: 3g; Fiber: 1g; Sugar: 2g; Cholesterol: 11mg

Greek Yogurt Deviled Eggs

Prep Time: 15 minutes | Cook Time: 15 minutes | Serves: 4

4 eggs
¼ cup nonfat plain Greek yogurt
1 teaspoon chopped fresh dill
⅛ teaspoon salt
⅛ teaspoon paprika
⅛ teaspoon garlic powder
Chopped fresh parsley, for garnish

1. Preheat the air fryer to 260°F.
2. Place the eggs in one layer in the air fryer basket and cook for 15 minutes.
3. Quickly remove the eggs from the air fryer and place them into a cold water bath. Let the eggs cool in the water for 10 minutes before removing and peeling them.
4. After peeling the eggs, cut them in half.
5. Spoon the yolk into a small bowl. Add the yogurt, dill, salt, paprika, and garlic powder and mix until smooth.
6. Fill the egg white halves with the yolk mixture using a spoon or piping bag. Garnish with a sprinkle of fresh parsley before serving.

Per Serving: Calories: 80; Total Fat: 5g; Saturated Fat: 2g; Protein: 8g; Total Carbohydrates: 1g; Fiber: 0g; Sugar: 1g; Cholesterol: 187mg

Spicy Roasted Chickpeas

Prep Time: 5 minutes | Cook Time: 30 minutes | Serves: 6

1 can low-sodium chickpeas (drained and rinsed, about 1½ cups)
½ teaspoon chili powder
½ teaspoon smoked paprika
¼ teaspoon garlic powder
1 spray olive oil (about 1 second spray)

1. Preheat the oven to 400°F. Pat the chickpeas dry with a paper towel.
2. Lightly spray with olive oil, then toss with spices until evenly coated. Spread on a baking sheet.
3. Roast for 25-30 minutes, stirring occasionally, until crispy. Let cool before serving.

Per Serving: Calories 45; Fat 0.8g; Sodium 12mg; Carbs 7.5g; Fiber 2.1g; Sugar 0.3g; Protein 2.4g

Sea Salt Beet Chips

Prep Time: 10 minutes | Cook Time: 30 minutes | Serves: 6

4 medium beets, rinse and sliced thin
1 teaspoon sea salt
2 tablespoons olive oil
Hummus, for serving

1. Preheat the air fryer to 380°F.
2. In a large bowl, toss the beets with sea salt and olive oil until well coated.
3. Put the beet slices into the air fryer and spread them out in a single layer.
4. Fry for 10 minutes. Stir, then fry for an additional 10 minutes. Stir again, then fry for a final 5 to 10 minutes, or until the chips reach the desired crispiness.
5. Serve with a favorite hummus.
Per Serving: Calories: 63; Total Fat: 5g; Saturated Fat: 1g; Protein: 1g; Total Carbohydrates: 5g; Fiber: 2g; Sugar: 3g; Cholesterol: 0mg

Garlic Cauliflower Puree

Prep Time: 20 minutes | Cook Time: 15 minutes | Serves: 12

6 cups raw cauliflower florets
4 tablespoons avocado or olive oil
6 whole cloves garlic
4 cloves garlic, crushed
6 tablespoons lemon juice
6 tablespoons extra virgin olive oil
4 tablespoons water
3 tablespoons tahini paste
¼ tsp smoked paprika plus some to garnish
Extra-virgin olive oil to drizzle
1½ teaspoons kosher salt

1. Add cauliflower, avocado oil, 1 teaspoon kosher salt, water and whole garlic cloves into a microwave-safe dish. Microwave on high for 15 minutes or until soft.
2. Remove from the microwave and cool for a while. Transfer into a blender.
3. Add the rest of the ingredients. Blend for 30-40 seconds or until smooth.
4. Transfer into a bowl. Taste and adjust the salt and paprika if required.
5. Sprinkle some paprika on top. Drizzle extra-virgin olive oil over it.
6. Serve with thin apple slices, vegetable sticks or celery sticks. Nutritional values of apple, celery, and vegetable sticks not included.
Per Serving: Calories 127; Fat 12.07g; Sodium 308mg; Carbs 4.84g; Fiber 1.2g; Sugar 1.85g; Protein 1.37g

Crisp Kale Chips

Prep Time: 12 minutes | Cook Time: 5 minutes | Serves: 6

6 cups kale, de-stemmed and torn into smaller pieces
2 tbsp. olive oil
2 tsp. onion powder
1 tsp. garlic powder
1 tsp. chili powder
½ tsp. salt
½ tsp. pepper

1. After prepping the kale, toss it in the spices and the olive oil until it's well-coated. Then, add the kale to the basket of the air fryer.
2. Cook the kale chips in the air fryer at 380°F for 5 minutes. Shake the basket every minute or so.
3. Serve the kale chips crispy and enjoy.
Per Serving: Calories 54; Fat 4.73g; Sodium 214mg; Carbs 2.76g; Fiber 1g; Sugar 0.46g; Protein 0.93g

Spicy Cauliflower

Prep Time: 10 minutes | Cook Time: 15 minutes | Serves: 6

1 head cauliflower, sliced into florets
2 tsp. garlic powder
1 tbsp. olive oil
½ tsp. pepper
½ tsp. salt
1 tbsp. coconut oil
½ cup Frank's hot sauce

1. Preheat the air fryer to 450°F. Place the cauliflower in a plastic bag. Add the olive oil, and shake the cauliflower to coat it.
2. Add the garlic powder, salt, and the pepper. Close the bag and shake it well. The cauliflower should be coated in spices.
3. Place the cauliflower into the air fryer. Cook the florets for 10 minutes, shaking the air fryer basket every two minutes to ensure they get crispy–but don't stick together.
4. Take the florets out of the air fryer. Meanwhile, melt the coconut oil in a glass bowl using the microwave or stovetop. Once melted, mix in the hot sauce and stir thoroughly.
5. Toss the cauliflower in the hot sauce mixture, coating it well.
6. Place the cauliflower back in the air fryer. Cook for 5 more minutes, shaking in the air fryer every minute or so. Serve warm, and enjoy.
Per Serving: Calories 75; Fat 4.84g; Sodium 377mg; Carbs 7.43g; Fiber 2.5g; Sugar 2.94g; Protein 2.46g

Mint Grapefruit Salad

Prep Time: 15 minutes | Serves: 4

2 tbsp. chopped cashews
½ cup coconut flakes
2 grapefruit
½ minced shallot
⅓ cup mint leaves
1 tbsp. minced shrimp
½ minced jalapeno
Juice from a lime
½ juiced orange
1 tbsp. fish sauce

1. Heat up a pan on the stove. When it becomes hot, toss the cashews and coconut flakes inside.
2. Let these toast for about 5 minutes and then take out of the pan to cool down before you continue.
3. Over a bowl catch the juice of the grapefruit and then get the juice from the membranes. Section the fruit and then get rid of the membranes so that you just have the fruit. Place into the bowl.
4. In another bowl, you can whisk the orange juice, fish sauce, lime juice, jalapeno, shrimp, shallot, and mint. Add the grapefruit and then fold to combine. Sprinkle with the cashews and coconut and then fold again.
5. Allow to set for 10 minutes to let it all mix together before you start to eat the snack.
Per Serving: Calories 163; Fat 7.48g; Sodium 425mg; Carbs 23.93g; Fiber 3.5g; Sugar 14.63g; Protein 3.25g

Mini Crab Cakes

Prep Time: 10 minutes | Cook Time: 10 minutes | Serves: 6

8 ounces lump crab meat
2 tablespoons diced red bell pepper
1 scallion, white parts and green parts, diced
1 garlic clove, minced
1 tablespoon capers, minced
1 tablespoon nonfat plain Greek yogurt
1 egg, beaten
¼ cup whole wheat bread crumbs
¼ teaspoon salt
1 tablespoon olive oil
1 lemon, cut into wedges

1. Preheat the air fryer to 360°F.
2. In a medium bowl, mix the crab, bell pepper, scallion, garlic, and capers until combined.
3. Add the yogurt and egg. Stir until incorporated. Mix in the bread crumbs and salt.
4. Divide this mixture into 6 equal portions and pat out into patties. Place the crab cakes into the air fryer basket in a single layer, making sure that they don't touch each other. Brush the tops of each patty with a bit of olive oil.
5. Bake for 10 minutes.
6. Remove the crab cakes from the air fryer and serve with lemon wedges on the side.

Per Serving: Calories: 87; Total Fat: 4g; Saturated Fat: 1g; Protein: 9g; Total Carbohydrates: 4g; Fiber: 0g; Sugar: 1g; Cholesterol: 61mg

Cucumber Yogurt Dip

Prep Time: 10 minutes | Serves: 8

1 cup fat-free Greek yogurt
1 cucumber, peeled, seeded, and finely chopped
1 tablespoon fresh dill, chopped
1 teaspoon lemon juice
½ teaspoon garlic powder
¼ teaspoon black pepper
Celery sticks or bell pepper strips, for dipping

1. Place the chopped cucumber in a clean kitchen towel and squeeze out excess moisture.
2. In a bowl, combine the yogurt, cucumber, dill, garlic powder, lemon juice, and black pepper. Mix well.
3. Refrigerate for 1 hour before serving with veggie sticks

Per Serving: Calories 22; Fat 0.1g; Sodium 15mg; Carbs 2.3g; Fiber 0.3g; Sugar 1.8g; Protein 3g

Shrimp and Dill Cucumber Bites

Prep Time: 15 minutes | Serves: 12

12 cucumber slices, cut ½-inch thick
12 cooked shrimp, peeled and deveined
2 tablespoons fat-free Greek yogurt
½ teaspoon lemon zest
½ teaspoon fresh dill, chopped
Black pepper, to taste

1. In a bowl, mix yogurt, lemon zest, dill, and black pepper.
2. Spoon the mixture onto each cucumber slice. Top each with shrimp and chill for 10 minutes before serving.

Per Serving: Calories 18; Fat 0.1g; Sodium 22mg; Carbs 0.8g; Fiber 0.2g; Sugar 0.3g; Protein 3.1g

Mini Zucchini & Tomato Frittatas

Prep Time: 10 minutes | Cook Time: 20 minutes | Serves: 12

4 egg whites + 1 whole egg
½ cup grated zucchini, squeeze out moisture
¼ cup cherry tomatoes, chopped or sliced
1 tablespoon chives, chopped
Olive oil spray, for greasing

1. Preheat the oven to 350°F. Lightly spray a mini muffin tin with olive oil.
2. In a bowl, whisk together eggs, zucchini, tomatoes, and chives. Pour into muffin cups, filling each ⅔ full.
3. Bake for 18-20 minutes until set. Let cool before removing from the tin.
Per Serving: Calories 20; Fat 0.6g; Sodium 18mg; Carbs 0.7g; Fiber 0.2g; Sugar 0.4g; Protein 2.9g

Turkey Spinach Pinwheels

Prep Time: 15 minutes | Serves: 10

2 low-carb whole wheat tortillas
4 slices low-sodium turkey breast
½ cup baby spinach leaves
2 tablespoons low-fat cream cheese
½ teaspoon Dijon mustard

1. Mix cream cheese and mustard, then spread evenly over the tortillas.
2. Layer turkey slices and spinach on top. Roll tightly and slice into ½-inch pinwheels.
Per Serving: Calories 38; Fat 1.2g; Sodium 85mg; Carbs 3.5g; Fiber 0.8g; Sugar 0.3g; Protein 3.8g

Edamame & Purple Cabbage Salad

Prep Time: 10 minutes | Serves: 8

1 cup shelled edamame, steamed
¼ cup shredded purple cabbage
2 tablespoons rice vinegar
1 teaspoon low-sodium soy sauce
½ teaspoon grated ginger
8 large lettuce leaves (e.g., romaine or butter lettuce)

1. In a bowl, combine edamame, cabbage, rice vinegar, soy sauce, and ginger. Stir to mix well.
2. Spoon the mixture into lettuce leaves and serve chilled. Sprinkle with sesame seeds if desired.
Per Serving: Calories 35; Fat 1.1g; Sodium 45mg; Carbs 3.2g; Fiber 1.5g; Sugar 0.4g; Protein 3.5g

Lemon White Bean Dip

Prep Time: 10 minutes | Serves: 10

1 can low-sodium white beans, drained and rinsed, about 1½ cups
1 tablespoon lemon juice
1 teaspoon lemon zest
1 garlic clove
½ teaspoon dried basil
2-3 tablespoons water, to adjust consistency
Cucumber slices, for dipping

1. Combine all the ingredients in a food processor and blend until the mixture is smooth and well combined. Add water as needed for desired consistency.
2. Chill for 1 hour before serving with cucumber slices.
Per Serving: Calories 40; Fat 0.3g; Sodium 10mg; Carbs 7.2g; Fiber 2g; Sugar 0.2g; Protein 2.5g

Chicken and Apple Salad

Prep Time: 20 minutes | Serves: 2

Zest and juice of ½ lemon
4 tablespoons thick, nonfat Greek yogurt
2 cooked skinless chicken breasts, weighing about 240g (8½oz), shredded
1 tablespoon dill, roughly chopped
1 small apple, unpeeled and roughly chopped
1 heart of celery or 2 celery sticks with leaves, finely chopped
1 tablespoon extra-virgin olive oil
2 teaspoons red wine vinegar
4 firm lettuce leaves, such as Romaine, or 6 Little Gem leaves
Salt and freshly ground black pepper

1. In a small bowl, combine the lemon zest, lemon juice, and yogurt, then season to taste. Divide the mixture in half and spoon it into two shallow bowls or plates, forming a small pile in each.
2. Mix all the remaining ingredients, except for the lettuce, and season to taste. Transfer to the 2 bowls, laying it next to the lemon yogurt, and serve with the lettuce on the side.

Per Serving: Calories 330; Fat 18g; Sodium 250mg; Carbs 13g; Fiber 4g; Sugar 8g; Protein 32g

Vegetable-Barley Salad

Prep Time: 25 minutes | Cook Time: 25 minutes | Serves: 6

1 cup water
½ cup pearl barley
4 cups chopped Brussels sprouts, roasted
3 celery stalks, chopped
2 carrots, chopped
1 yellow bell pepper, seeded and chopped
2 cups chopped cauliflower, steamed
1 cup halved cherry tomatoes
¼ cup roasted, unsalted pumpkin seeds
1 scallion, both white and green parts, chopped
¼ cup extra-virgin olive oil
Juice of 1 lemon
Sea salt
Freshly ground black pepper

1. In a small saucepan, combine the water and barley and bring to a boil over medium-high heat. Cover, reduce the heat to low, and simmer for 22 to 25 minutes, until tender but with a bit of bite.
2. While the barley is cooking, in a large bowl, toss together the Brussels sprouts, celery, carrots, bell pepper, cauliflower, tomatoes, pumpkin seeds, and scallion until well mixed.
3. In a small bowl, whisk together the oil and lemon juice, then season with salt and pepper.
4. Add the cooked barley and dressing to the salad, toss to combine, and serve.

Per Serving: Calories 167; Fat 3.93g; Sodium 705mg; Carbs 30.05g; Fiber 7.4g; Sugar 6.57g; Protein 6.85g

Butternut Squash and Carrot Salad

Prep Time: 30 minutes | Serves: 4

For the Dressing:
¼ cup extra-virgin olive oil
3 tablespoons apple cider vinegar
1 tablespoon maple syrup
1 teaspoon peeled and grated fresh ginger
For the Salad:
½ small butternut squash, shredded
¼ head red cabbage, shredded
2 carrots, shredded
1 apple, cored and chopped
2 scallions, both white and green parts, thinly sliced
1 tablespoon chopped fresh thyme

To make the dressing:
1. In a small bowl, whisk together the oil, vinegar, maple syrup, and ginger until well blended. Set aside.
To make the salad:
1. In a large bowl, toss the squash, red cabbage, carrots, apple, scallions, and thyme until well mixed.
2. Add the dressing, toss, and serve.
Per Serving: Calories: 252; Total fat: 17g; Saturated fat: 2g; Sodium: 130mg; Carbohydrates: 24g; Sugar: 17g; Fiber: 4g; Protein: 2g

Roasted Red Pepper and Basil Soup

Prep Time: 20 minutes | Cook Time: 35 minutes | Serves: 4

4 red bell peppers
1 tablespoon olive oil
2 large onions, chopped (2 cups)
3 cloves garlic, sliced
2 cups vegetable broth or low-sodium chicken broth
1 cup water
¼ teaspoon cracked black pepper
1 cup thinly sliced fresh basil leaves
½ yellow bell pepper, diced
8 small (cherry-size) fat-free mozzarella balls, quartered
4 slices crusty multigrain or whole wheat bread

1. Set oven control to broil. On rack in broiler pan, place red bell peppers. roil the peppers with the tops about 5 inches from the heat for 10 to 15 minutes, turning occasionally, until the skin is blistered and evenly browned. Transfer the roasted bell peppers to a large bowl, cover with plastic wrap, and let them stand for 15 minutes.
2. Meanwhile, heat the oil over medium-low heat in a 4-quart saucepan. Add the onions and garlic to the oil and cook for 7 to 9 minutes, stirring occasionally, until the onions begin to brown. Remove from heat.
3. Remove skin, stems, seeds and membranes from roasted bell peppers; cut bell peppers into strips. Into onion mixture, stir bell pepper strips, broth, water and pepper. Heat to boiling; reduce heat. Simmer uncovered 10 minutes, stirring occasionally; stir in ½ cup of the basil.
4. In a blender or food processor, place about one-third of the soup mixture. Cover and blend on high speed until smooth, stopping to scrape down the sides of the blender as needed. Pour into a large bowl. Repeat with the remaining soup mixture in two more batches.
5. Divide soup evenly among 4 bowls. To serve, top soup with diced yellow bell pepper and the mozzarella; sprinkle with remaining basil. Serve with bread.
Per Serving: Calories 200; Total Fat 6g (Saturated Fat 1.5g; Trans Fat 0g); Cholesterol 0mg; Sodium 620mg; Total Carbohydrate 29g (Dietary Fiber 6g; Sugars 13g); Protein 7g

Artichoke Hearts and Chickpeas Salad

Prep Time: 20 minutes | Serves: 6

For the Salad:
1 head Bibb lettuce or ½ head romaine lettuce, chopped (about 2½ cups)
¼ cup loosely packed chopped basil leaves
1 (15-ounce) can chickpeas, drained and rinsed
1 (14-ounce) can artichoke hearts, drained and halved
1 pint grape tomatoes, halved (about 1½ cups)
1 seedless cucumber, peeled and chopped (about 1½ cups)
½ cup cubed feta cheese (about 2 ounces)
1 (2.25-ounce) can sliced black olives (about ½ cup)
For the Dressing:
3 tablespoons extra-virgin olive oil
1 tablespoon red wine vinegar
1 tablespoon freshly squeezed lemon juice (from about ½ small lemon)
1 tablespoon chopped fresh oregano or ½ teaspoon dried oregano
1 teaspoon honey
¼ teaspoon freshly ground black pepper

To make the salad:
1. In a medium bowl, toss the lettuce and basil together. Spread out on a large serving platter or in a large salad bowl.
2. Arrange the chickpeas, artichoke hearts, cucumber, tomatoes, feta, and olives in piles next to each other on top of the lettuce layer.
To make the dressing:
1. In a small pitcher or bowl, whisk together the oil, oregano, vinegar, lemon juice, honey, and pepper.
2. Serve on the side with the salad, or drizzle over all the ingredients right before serving.
Per Serving: Calories: 226; Total Fat: 13g; Saturated Fat: 3g; Cholesterol: 11mg; Sodium: 545mg; Total Carbohydrates: 23g; Fiber: 8g; Protein: 8g

Beef, Mushroom and Cabbage Soup

Prep Time: 15 minutes | Cook Time: 40 minutes | Serves: 4

6 cups beef or vegetable stock, all organic, store-bought, unsalted
2 large garlic cloves, minced
1 large celery rib, strings removed, minced
1 large shallot, minced
1 piece small carrots, peeled, diced
1 can (15 oz.) button mushrooms, pieces, and stems, rinsed well, drained
1 tbsp. olive oil
½ head white cabbage, cored, tough stems removed, julienned
½ pound lean ground beef
sea salt and white pepper to taste
For Garnish: (all optional)
⅛ cup fresh chives, minced
A dash of dried pepper flakes

1. Pour oil into a Dutch oven set over medium heat.
2. Add in and sauté garlic and onion until limp and aromatic. Add in ground beef; stir-fry until seared brown, breaking up larger clumps as you go. Except for garnishes and cabbage, add in remaining ingredients into Dutch oven. Stir.
3. Bring soup to a boil. Secure lid. Turn down heat to lowest setting. Simmer for 20 minutes.
4. Add cabbage. Cook for another 10 minutes, covered. Taste; adjust seasoning, if needed. Turn off heat.
5. Ladle soup into bowls. Garnish with fresh chives and pepper flakes, if using. Cool soup slightly before serving.
Per Serving: Calories 329; Fat 12.98g; Sodium 626mg; Carbs 28.27g; Fiber 7.7g; Sugar 7.87g; Protein 26.75g

Broccoli Ginger Soup

Prep Time: 10 minutes | Cook Time: 3 hours | Serves: 6

1 tsp. turmeric
8 cups broccoli florets
1 tbsp. sesame oil
6 cups chicken stock
2 tbsp. ginger – shredded
Optional:
Sea salt and pepper

1. Add all the ingredients to the slow cooker. Cover and cook on low for 3 hours, or until the broccoli becomes tender.
2. When the time is up, use a hand or immersion blender to blend the soup to a desired consistency or until smooth. Serve with fresh microgreens.
Per Serving: Calories 121; Fat 5.44g; Sodium 439mg; Carbs 10.68g; Fiber 1.6g; Sugar 4.04g; Protein 7.82g

Citrus Kale Salad

Prep Time: 15 minutes | Cook Time: 10 minutes | Serves: 4

2 tablespoons toasted sesame seeds
1 tablespoon extra-virgin olive oil
8 cups kale leaves, stems removed and roughly torn
¼ cup pumpkin seeds, raw, shelled, and unsalted
1 orange, peeled and cut into segments
1 grapefruit, peeled and cut into segments
1 cup tahini dressing

1. If your sesame seeds are not pre-toasted, place them in a dry medium skillet over medium heat. Toast for 2 to 3 minutes, or until they start to brown slightly and become fragrant. Remove them from the pan.
2. In the same pan, heat the olive oil over medium heat. Add 4 cups of kale and cook undisturbed for about 1 minute, then lightly toss and cook for about 1 minute more, charring it slightly.
3. Remove the kale from the pan to a serving plate and set aside. Repeat the process with the remaining 2 cups of kale, adding it to the plate.
4. Top the charred kale with the toasted sesame seeds, pumpkin seeds, orange segments, and grapefruit segments.
5. Drizzle the Tahini Dressing over the salad and serve.
Per Serving: Calories: 372; Total fat: 32g; Saturated fat: 5g; Sodium: 45mg; Carbohydrates: 19g; Fiber: 6g; Sugar: 9g; Protein: 8g

Orange and Celery Salad

Prep Time: 15 minutes | Serves: 6

3 celery stalks, including leaves, sliced diagonally into ½-inch slices
2 large oranges, peeled and sliced into rounds
½ cup green olives (or any variety)
¼ cup sliced red onion (about ¼ onion)
1 tablespoon extra-virgin olive oil
1 tablespoon olive brine
1 tablespoon freshly squeezed lemon or orange juice (from ½ small lemon or 1 orange round)
¼ teaspoon kosher or sea salt
¼ teaspoon freshly ground black pepper

1. Place the celery, oranges, olives, and onion on a large serving platter or in a shallow, wide bowl.
2. In a small bowl, whisk together the oil, olive brine, and lemon juice. Pour over the salad, sprinkle with salt and pepper, and serve.
Per Serving: Calories: 65; Total Fat: 4g; Saturated Fat: 0g; Cholesterol: 0mg; Sodium: 258mg; Total Carbohydrates: 9g; Fiber: 3g; Protein: 2g

Simple Egg Drop Soup

Prep Time: 10 minutes | Cook Time: 15 minutes | Serves: 4

3½ cups low-sodium vegetable broth, divided
1 teaspoon grated fresh ginger (optional)
2 garlic cloves, minced
3 teaspoons low-sodium soy sauce or tamari
1 tablespoon cornstarch
2 large eggs, lightly beaten
2 scallions, both white and green parts, thinly sliced

1. In a large saucepan, bring 3 cups plus 6 tablespoons of vegetable broth and the ginger (if using), garlic, and tamari to a boil over medium-high heat.
2. In a small bowl, make a slurry by combining the cornstarch and the remaining 2 tablespoons of broth. Stir until dissolved. Gradually pour the cornstarch mixture into the heated soup, stirring constantly until it thickens, about 2 to 3 minutes.
3. Reduce the heat to low and simmer. While stirring the soup, pour the eggs in slowly. Turn off the heat, add the scallions, and serve.

Per Serving: Calories: 66; Total fat: 3g; Carbohydrates: 6g; Fiber: 1g; Protein: 4g; Calcium: 40mg; Vitamin D: 1mcg; Vitamin B12: <1mcg; Iron: 1mg; Zinc: <1mg

Turkey, Cauliflower and Kale Soup

Prep Time: 15 minutes | Cook Time: 25 minutes | Serves: 3

½ pound ground turkey
2 medium carrots, peeled, sliced
2 shallots, chopped
1 small bell pepper, chopped
¾ cup cauliflower, minced
2½ cups chicken stock
1 tablespoon coconut oil
2 cups kale, discard hard ribs and stems, chopped
Sea salt to taste
Pepper to taste

1. Place a saucepan over medium-high heat. Add oil. When the oil melts, add shallots, bell pepper, cauliflower, and carrots. Sauté until slightly soft.
2. Add ground turkey and cook until brown. Break it into smaller pieces simultaneously as it cooks.
3. Add rest of the ingredients except kale and stir. Bring to the boil.
4. Add kale and stir. Lower heat and cover with a lid. Simmer until kale turns bright green in color.
5. Ladle into soup bowls and serve.

Per Serving: Calories 264; Fat 13.56g; Sodium 613mg; Carbs 15.91g; Fiber 2.6g; Sugar 7.13g; Protein 21.04g

Roasted Red Pepper and Tomato Soup

Prep Time: 15 minutes | Cook Time: 20 minutes | Serves: 4

1 carrot, peeled, chopped
1 medium onion, chopped
1 stalk celery, chopped
2 cloves garlic, minced
7 ounces roasted red peppers in water
36 ounces canned whole tomatoes with its juice
2 cups vegetable broth
1 bay leaf
A handful fresh basil, chopped
Salt to taste
Pepper to taste

1. Add all the ingredients into a soup pot or Dutch oven.
2. Cook until tender. Discard bay leaf.
3. Use an immersion blender to blend until smooth. Alternately, you can blend in a blender.
4. Ladle into soup bowls and serve.

Per Serving: Calories 120; Fat 1.94g; Sodium 1204mg; Carbs 23.7g; Fiber 4g; Sugar 12.14g; Protein 5.32g

Feta Cucumber Salad

For the Salad:
1 head romaine lettuce, torn
½ cup black olives, pitted and chopped
1 red onion, thinly sliced
1 tomato, chopped
1 cucumber, chopped
½ cup crumbled feta cheese
For the Dressing:
2 tablespoons extra-virgin olive oil
2 tablespoons red wine vinegar
Juice of 1 lemon
1 tablespoon dried oregano (or 2 tablespoons chopped fresh oregano leaves)
3 garlic cloves, minced
½ teaspoon Dijon mustard
½ teaspoon sea salt
¼ teaspoon freshly ground black pepper

1. To make the salad, in a large bowl, mix the lettuce, red onion, olives, tomato, cucumber, and feta.
2. To make the dressing, in a small bowl, whisk the olive oil, vinegar, lemon juice, oregano, garlic, mustard, sea salt, and pepper.
3. To assemble, just before serving, toss the salad with the dressing.
Per Serving: Calories: 203; Protein: 15g; Total Carbohydrates: 13g; Sugars: 5g; Fiber: 3g; Total Fat: 15g; Saturated Fat: 6g; Cholesterol: 25mg; Sodium: 716mg

Chicken and Vegetable Salad

2 heads romaine lettuce, chopped
3 cups chopped skinless cooked chicken breast
1 cup canned or jarred (in water) artichoke hearts, drained, rinsed, and chopped
12 cherry tomatoes, chopped
2 zucchinis, chopped
½ red onion, finely chopped
3 ounces fat-free mozzarella cheese, chopped
⅓ cup unsweetened nonfat plain Greek yogurt
1 tablespoon Dijon mustard
2 tablespoons extra-virgin olive oil
Zest of 1 lemon
3 garlic cloves, minced
2 tablespoons chopped fresh basil leaves
2 tablespoons chopped fresh chives
½ teaspoon sea salt
⅛ teaspoon freshly ground black pepper

1. In a large bowl, combine the lettuce, chicken, artichoke hearts, red onion, cherry tomatoes, zucchini, and mozzarella.
2. In a small bowl, whisk the yogurt, mustard, lemon zest, garlic, olive oil, basil, chives, sea salt, and pepper.
3. Toss the dressing with the salad before serving.
Per Serving: Calories: 302; Protein: 29g; Total Carbohydrates: 14g; Sugars: 5g; Fiber: 5g; Total Fat: 15g; Saturated Fat: 4g; Cholesterol: 71mg; Sodium: 480mg

Salmon and Blueberry Salad

Prep Time: 15 minutes | Cook Time: 10 minutes | Serves: 4

Pepper to taste
Salt to taste
1 tbsp. olive oil
½ cup halved grape tomatoes
¼ cup blueberries
1 sliced avocado
1 salmon fillet
1½ cup chopped kale
1½ cup spinach

1. Start by placing the chopped kale and spinach into a large bowl. Toss them gently to combine, ensuring they are evenly mixed. These greens will form the base of your salad.
2. Heat a non-stick skillet over medium heat. Once hot, add 1 tablespoon of olive oil and swirl to coat the pan. Season both sides of the salmon fillet with salt and pepper. Place the salmon in the skillet and cook for about 4-5 minutes on each side, or until the salmon flakes easily when tested with a fork. If you prefer your salmon well done, cook it for an additional 2-3 minutes.
3. While the salmon is cooking, halve the grape tomatoes and place them in the bowl with the greens. Add the blueberries and sliced avocado as well. These ingredients will add flavor and color to the salad.
4. Once the salmon is cooked, remove it from the skillet and let it rest for a minute or two. Use a fork to break the salmon into bite-sized pieces. Add the flaked salmon to the salad mixture, gently tossing to incorporate all the ingredients.
5. Season the salad with additional salt and pepper to taste, and serve immediately for a fresh, healthy, and nutrient-packed meal.
Per Serving: Calories 235; Fat 14.44g; Sodium 367mg; Carbs 9.67g; Fiber 4.4g; Sugar 4.28g; Protein 18.18g

Turkey and Kale Soup

Prep Time: 10 minutes | Cook Time: 3 hours | Serves: 4

½ lb. kale, chopped
6 cups chicken broth
1 red bell pepper, diced
1 lb. turkey, cooked and shredded
4 tomatoes, diced
Optional:
Sea salt and pepper to taste
Fresh parsley, for garnish

1. Start by washing and chopping the kale into bite-sized pieces. Dice the red bell pepper and tomatoes. Shred the cooked turkey if it's not already done.
2. In a slow cooker, add the chopped kale, diced bell pepper, diced tomatoes, and shredded turkey. Pour the chicken broth into the mixture, stirring well to ensure everything is thoroughly combined.
3. If desired, season with sea salt and freshly ground pepper to taste, then stir once more to blend the seasonings into the soup.
4. Secure the slow cooker lid and set it to cook on high for 3 hours. As it cooks, the kale will become tender, and the flavors of the vegetables, turkey, and broth will blend harmoniously.
5. When the cooking time is up, portion the soup into bowls. Top each serving with fresh parsley for a vibrant touch and an extra layer of flavor.
Per Serving: Calories 260; Fat 6.16g; Sodium 931mg; Carbs 11.75g; Fiber 3.2g; Sugar 4g; Protein 40.08g

Lime Cucumber Yogurt Salad

Prep Time: 15 minutes | Serves: 4

3 English cucumbers, very thinly sliced
½ teaspoon sea salt
¼ red onion, thinly sliced
½ cup fat-free plain Greek yogurt
2 tablespoons chopped fresh mint, or 1 tablespoon dried mint
Juice and zest of 1 lime
1 tablespoon maple syrup
Freshly ground black pepper

1. Place the cucumber slices in a fine-mesh sieve and toss with the salt. Let the slices sit for 15 minutes to drain out the excess moisture.
2. Transfer the slices to a medium bowl and toss with the onion.
3. In a small bowl, whisk together the yogurt, mint, lime juice, lime zest, and maple syrup.
4. Add the dressing to the cucumber and toss to coat. Season with pepper and serve.

Per Serving: Calories: 62; Total fat: 0g; Saturated fat: 0g; Sodium: 94mg; Carbohydrates: 11g; Sugar: 7g; Fiber: 2g; Protein: 4g

Herbed Mushroom-Barley Soup

Prep Time: 15 minutes | Cook Time: 25 minutes | Serves: 6

2 tablespoons extra-virgin olive oil
1 cup chopped onion (about ½ medium onion)
1 cup chopped carrots (about 2 carrots)
5½ cups chopped mushrooms (about 12 ounces)
6 cups low-sodium or no-salt-added vegetable broth
1 cup uncooked pearled barley
2 tablespoons tomato paste
½ teaspoon dried thyme or 4 sprigs fresh thyme
1 dried bay leaf
6 tablespoons grated Parmesan cheese

1. In a large stockpot over medium heat, heat the oil. Add the onion and carrots and cook for 5 minutes, stirring frequently. Turn up the heat to medium-high and add the mushrooms. Cook for 3 minutes, stirring frequently.
2. Add the broth, barley, tomato paste, thyme, and bay leaf. Stir, cover the pot, and bring the soup to a boil. Once it's boiling, stir a few times, reduce the heat to medium-low, cover, and cook for another 12 to 15 minutes, until the barley is cooked through.
3. Remove the bay leaf and serve in soup bowls with 1 tablespoon of cheese sprinkled on top of each.

Per Serving: Calories: 236; Total Fat: 7g; Saturated Fat: 2g; Cholesterol: 5mg; Sodium: 231mg; Total Carbohydrates: 35g; Fiber: 7g; Protein: 8g

Conclusion

The Dr. Now 1200-Calorie Diet Plan for Beginners offers an effective, structured, and sustainable approach to weight loss, making it ideal for individuals looking to improve their health while shedding excess pounds. This diet is not just about reducing calories; it's about making smarter food choices that prioritize nutrient-dense options while limiting unhealthy, processed foods.

Through a carefully planned 1200-calorie intake, the Dr. Now diet helps create a calorie deficit necessary for weight loss, but it does so in a way that promotes overall health. By focusing on lean proteins, non-starchy vegetables, healthy fats, and whole grains, this plan ensures that your body gets the nutrients it needs without the excess calories. Plus, the diet encourages habits that can lead to better blood sugar control, improved metabolic rate, and sustained weight management.

It simplifies the meal planning process, providing a wide variety of easy-to-follow recipes that are both delicious and nutritious. Whether you're a beginner or someone more experienced in the kitchen, this cookbook will guide you through the essential steps, helping you make the most out of every meal. With helpful tips, a meal plan, and simple recipes, this guide ensures that you stay on track and motivated to reach your health goals.

By incorporating the Dr. Now 1200-Calorie Diet into your lifestyle, you'll not only lose weight but also cultivate a healthier, more balanced relationship with food. If you're looking to make lasting, positive changes, this plan and cookbook are the perfect starting point.

Appendix 1 Measurement Conversion Chart

VOLUME EQUIVALENTS (LIQUID)

US STANDARD	US STANDARD (OUNCES)	METRIC (APPROXIMATE)
2 tablespoons	1 fl.oz	30 mL
¼ cup	2 fl.oz	60 mL
½ cup	4 fl.oz	120 mL
1 cup	8 fl.oz	240 mL
1½ cup	12 fl.oz	355 mL
2 cups or 1 pint	16 fl.oz	475 mL
4 cups or 1 quart	32 fl.oz	1 L
1 gallon	128 fl.oz	4 L

VOLUME EQUIVALENTS (DRY)

US STANDARD	METRIC (APPROXIMATE)
⅛ teaspoon	0.5 mL
¼ teaspoon	1 mL
½ teaspoon	2 mL
¾ teaspoon	4 mL
1 teaspoon	5 mL
1 tablespoon	15 mL
¼ cup	59 mL
½ cup	118 mL
¾ cup	177 mL
1 cup	235 mL
2 cups	475 mL
3 cups	700 mL
4 cups	1 L

TEMPERATURES EQUIVALENTS

FAHRENHEIT(F)	CELSIUS(C) (APPROXIMATE)
225 °F	107 °C
250 °F	120 °C
275 °F	135 °C
300 °F	150 °C
325 °F	160 °C
350 °F	180 °C
375 °F	190 °C
400 °F	205 °C
425 °F	220 °C
450 °F	235 °C
475 °F	245 °C
500 °F	260 °C

WEIGHT EQUIVALENTS

US STANDARD	METRIC (APPROXINATE)
1 ounce	28 g
2 ounces	57 g
5 ounces	142 g
10 ounces	284 g
15 ounces	425 g
16 ounces (1 pound)	455 g
1.5 pounds	680 g
2 pounds	907 g

Appendix 2 Recipes Index

Made in United States
Troutdale, OR
05/04/2025

30977086R00042